Solfege
and
Sonority

SOLFEGE AND SONORITY: TEACHING MUSIC READING IN THE CHORAL CLASSROOM

DAVID J. XIQUES

OXFORD
UNIVERSITY PRESS

OXFORD
UNIVERSITY PRESS

Oxford University Press is a department of the University of
Oxford. It furthers the University's objective of excellence in
research, scholarship, and education by publishing worldwide.

Oxford   New York
Auckland   Cape Town   Dar es Salaam   Hong Kong   Karachi
Kuala Lumpur   Madrid   Melbourne   Mexico City   Nairobi
New Delhi   Shanghai   Taipei   Toronto

With offices in
Argentina   Austria   Brazil   Chile   Czech Republic   France   Greece
Guatemala   Hungary   Italy   Japan   Poland   Portugal   Singapore
South Korea   Switzerland   Thailand   Turkey   Ukraine   Vietnam

Library of Congress Cataloging-in-Publication Data
Xiques, David J.
Solfege and sonority : teaching music reading in treble
choral music / by David J. Xiques.
    pages   cm
Includes bibliographical references and index.
ISBN 978-0-19-994435-4 (pbk. : alk. paper) — ISBN 978-0-19-994431-6
(hardcover : alk. paper) 1. Music—Instruction and study. 2. Music theory.
3. Sight-reading (Music) 4. Sight-singing. 5. Tonic sol-fa. I. Title.
MT10.X57 2014
781.4'23—dc23   2013029240

Web examples (marked in text with 🔊) are available online at www.oup.com/us/musicalcreativity
Access with username Music1 and password Book5983
For more information on Oxford Web Music, visit www.oxfordwebmusic.com

9   8   7   6   5   4   3   2   1

Printed in the United States of America on acid-free paper

Dedicated to all those who want to know more about the art of teaching and the making of music.

CONTENTS

ACKNOWLEDGEMENTS

THIS BOOK BRINGS TOGETHER all that my many teachers and fellow musicians have passed on to me.

Thank you to all my public school teachers, who shared their love of music and dedication to the special art of teaching. I want to thank Luke Grubb and the other music professors at Millersville University of Pennsylvania, who first introduced me to Kodály and who held such high expectations for music and education. Audrey Sherrill did so much to develop my piano performance skills. Erzsébet Hegyi's teaching, books, and level of musicianship and pedagogy were truly inspiring. Rita Klinger and Edward Bolkavac helped me at Holy Names University to refine my own pedagogy, and my colleagues and students at San Francisco State University and New York University's Kodály Summer Institute helped me dialogue and learn about teaching at advanced levels. My sincere appreciation for Vance George, director emeritus of the San Francisco Symphony Chorus, who, as friend and mentor, taught me that music is so much more than the notes printed on the page.

Thank you to Joshua Habermann, Sara Johnson, and William Skaff, and all the incredible editors at Oxford University Press for proofreading my text. Special appreciation is due to Rebecca Bouc and Nick Bacchetto for helping me with the intricacies of formatting the musical examples.

And thank you to my dad and mom, Kenneth and Gloria Xiques, who bought my first piano, paid for lessons, and who gave me the support to take my first Kodály musicianship class.

ABOUT THE COMPANION WEBSITE

Oxford University Press has created a companion website that contains additional materials that correspond with lessons found in this book. the URL for the site is:

www.oup.com/us/solfegeandsonority
Username: Music2
Password: Book4416

Here you will find videos of some of the procedures found in this book. The videos include the actual teaching of children, peer teaching in a college choral conducting class, and a demo lesson taught by me to college students as part of their education in choral methodology. These lessons are marked in the book with this symbol: ⬤.

Also included on the website are supplemental melodic and rhythmic reading exercises for you to download, print out, and use with your singers. Feel free to make as many copies as you need. These materials are indicated marked in the book with this symbol: ⬤.

Solfege
and
Sonority

INTRODUCTION
PURPOSE

AS CONDUCTORS AND EXPERIENCED performers, we often take our hard-earned musical reading skills for granted. We rely on our training to aid us in getting to the printed score quickly, and we value members of our ensembles who can do the same through their own training.

Yet in choral education, we have a conundrum. While we respect music literacy in our singers, they often come to us with little or no music reading skills. How, as educators, do we teach the extensive body of concert repertoire in limited time while simultaneously imparting reading skills?

Conductors should own their roles as teachers. We teach our singers by sequencing melodic and rhythmic elements, creating lesson plans, and excerpting short examples from the repertoire that we work on in rehearsals. These efforts save precious time, teach our members how to read, provide our singers with tools for their future involvement in choral ensembles, as well as continuing the development of the current performance repertoire.

We can and should teach musical interpretation and expression as well as music literacy in the choral rehearsal. We will best serve our students by enabling them to gain valuable music reading skills as we move away from a sole rote teaching approach. This is the goal of the approach in this book.

MUSIC AS A LANGUAGE

Zoltán Kodály (1882–1967), the great Hungarian composer, educator, ethnomusicologist, and philosopher, once said the most effective approach to musical reading training is to mimic the way we learned our native language. As young children, we learned to speak syllables that lead to words. As we grew, we learned to form those words into sentences, statements, and questions. We began holding conversations. We first learned what our language sounded like before we learned how to read and construct it.

Once we knew the sounds of language, teachers began to show us what the symbols of those sounds looked like in writing, a little at a time and in a very logical sequence. We began to study these symbols by reading simple words:

dog, cat, Dad, Mom. As our intellectual capacities grew, we learned longer words and began to write them and form them into larger sentences and paragraphs. Eventually, a teacher asked us to write short true stories, for example stories about what we did during summer vacation.

Finally, our teachers asked us to write stories from our own imaginations. We entered the realm of synthesis, the highest level of learning, the act of taking what we knew and creating our own stories. When we achieved this level of learning, creativity became part of us, part of our knowledge and skills.

This is the same process Kodály and other music educators embrace for the teaching of musical language. With younger singers we use quite a bit of rote learning at first. Older singers experience less rote learning since they are able to intellectualize more.

As we begin the process of teaching our students how to read music, we have to be careful that we don't try to teach too much all at once. In math we all want our students to be able to understand and perform long division. But first they must learn addition and subtraction with much practice and reinforcement. Taking one step at a time in a logical and sequenced manner leads to success.

HOW TO USE THIS BOOK

Organization of the Rehearsal

I recommend teaching the music reading procedures in the "ear" portion of your choral warm-up session. Since it is at the beginning of the rehearsal, your singers will be more receptive and energized. Their retention of the concepts will be better when the instruction is placed at the beginning of the rehearsal and not at the end when they may be more fatigued.

The following progression is an effective way to organize the warm-up:

> **Body**
> Posture, stretching, and relaxation activities
> **Breath**
> Exercises focusing on breathing technique and diaphragm activation
> **Voice**
> Vocalization, sighing, and proper production
> **Ear, or Ear-Training**
> Brief and meaningful activities that practice music literacy skills

Organization of the Melodic and Rhythmic Concepts

You will notice that melodic and rhythmic elements accompanied by suggested teaching procedures are interspersed throughout this text. This is due to the reality that we as teachers have to layer the concepts logically so that our singers quickly learn to put them together. After all, the goal is that our singers should be able to read melody and rhythm together. Take your time and make sure you do not try to do too much at once.

The order of the lessons is only a suggested sequence since the repertoire you have selected for your chorus will ultimately decide what you teach and when. Therefore, you should arrange the lessons in the order that makes the best sense for you and the repertoire you have chosen. Make sure that however you order the sequence, the concepts flow logically out of what your singers already know.

Each lesson begins with the overall idea and a summary of the melodic and rhythmic topic you will teach. You will also find an example of a folk song, a vocal warm-up, or an excerpt from a choral score to go with the lesson. Use the suggested example if it happens to be in your ensemble's repertoire, or find another that is similar. **Important:** It is much easier to teach new melodic tones and rhythms if the singers already know how to sing the music that you use to teach the concepts.

Many of the lessons contain a reinforcement activity or sight-reading lesson to show you how to move the new knowledge into the level of application. Finally, each lesson ends with a list of additional choral compositions that you can substitute for the ones already presented.

The lesson plans are written in two formats: narrative and descriptive. The narrative lessons provide specific questions and statements to lead the choristers through the learning process. The descriptive lessons provide the steps but require you to formulate your own questions and statements to the singers. For both formats, make sure to use your own logic and creativity in teaching to make the lesson as clear as possible to you and your ensemble. Feel free to change the language of the narrative lessons to "sound like you" and to fit your own creative teaching style.

One of the major goals of this type of instruction is to teach singers to read melody and rhythm from their own scores independently. Therefore, it is crucial that each procedure end with asking the singers to find and read the new element from their own printed music. Be sure to observe the ensemble so that you can inconspicuously help choristers who may have difficulty following the notation or who may be performing from memory and not actually reading the score.

It should be your goal to sing the words of the composition at the end of the instructive procedure. Always return to the text of the song. Making music as soon as possible should always be the goal of our teaching. Keeping this in mind makes our teaching more interesting for our singers and satisfying to us as musicians.

4

SUGGESTIONS FOR DIFFERENT USERS

Conductors

Read the strategies and study the pedagogy; then begin to find similar melodic and rhythmic patterns in the repertoire you have selected for your ensemble. Assess the base musical knowledge of your singers and start there, with what they already know. Move them from the "known" to the "unknown." Slowly and logically begin to add to their knowledge by asking them questions that encourage them to listen and think critically about the new concepts they encounter in their repertoire. And don't try to teach too much at once.

Teachers of Future Conductors

Study the strategies and sequence of materials so that you understand the logical flow of teaching this approach to music literacy. Find the places where it makes sense to you to adjust to your own style of teaching and incorporate your own creativity. Model a few of the strategies for your students and then ask them to select a few from this book to teach their peers during class time. One way our students learn is by copying their teachers. Once they understand the flow of this type of instruction, ask them to find their own choral scores and create their own lesson strategies to peer teach and to turn in as class assignments. Give critical but positive comments in your feedback when students peer teach and ask questions to lead the class to make corrections to help improve performance. As I learned from one of my master teachers, Rita Klinger, invite the student conductors to ask themselves, "Did the lesson work? If so, why did it work? If not, what can be improved to make the teaching procedure more effective?"

Students of Conducting and Music Pedagogy

Watch and participate fully when your teacher or fellow students teach the class according to the lessons in this text. Think critically while they teach you and ask yourself these questions:

- What is the teacher assuming that I already know?
- What are the logical and sequential steps that allowed me to learn the new concept?
- Was the selection of repertoire appropriate to the lesson?
- Is there something that I would add or change in the pedagogy to make it work better for me and for my way of thinking and teaching?
- What happened in the teaching procedure that made it successful so I can apply it in other lessons?

These questions are the same ones you should ask yourself when you are planning for teaching your own strategies.

Begin your teaching by using strategies as models almost exactly as they are written in this book. Then, as you begin to understand the logic, sequence, and pedagogy, start to create your own strategies using your own language and creativity.

Find conductors where you live who teach music literacy during their rehearsals and observe their techniques. Ask yourself the questions above as you critically view these conductors at work and write down the sequence of their strategies. Finding a mentor and emulating his or her skills will change your life!

Teachers of Older Beginners and General Music

The sequence of concepts and techniques described in this book's teaching strategies also works for teaching older beginners who are not in a choral ensemble. Simply replace the choral repertoire with other pieces of age-appropriate music, folk songs, and composed music, for example, and follow the logic demonstrated through the steps.

MUSIC VOCABULARY

THE BEST WAY TO BEGIN TEACHING musical reading is by using the musical language the students already have—the sounds of the melodies they already know. This body of repertoire includes folk songs, chants, and pop music. For example, while I was recently teaching a graduate conducting class at New York University, I observed a conductor teaching the following rhythm:

She shouted, "Let's go Yankees!" (She's from New York.) The Big Apple natives in the class responded automatically by stomping and clapping the rhythm above. By recalling the sounds the students already knew, she had created the foundation for teaching them the visual representations and names of the symbols for those sounds. They could then read quarter notes and eighth notes.

In choral rehearsals, you can rely on common musical repertoire ("Hot Cross Buns," "Three Blind Mice," etc.) and teach singers a new body of repertoire through other simple folk songs and vocal warm-ups. This material is a good starting place for reading.

MELODIC TOOLS

Music educators use either syllables or counting to teach and read rhythm. While you can use numbers for the degrees of the scale, moveable do solfa (also known as solfeggio, solfege, melody names) makes the most sense for singers since it is more beautiful to sing, is easier, and is a language that is unique to musicians. In moveable do, do-to-mi will always sound like a major third, regardless of the music's key. In fixed do, the letters C (do) through E (mi) sound like a major third, but C to E-flat is also called do and mi but sounds like a minor third.

While I believe solfa is the most effective method (and the method I use in this book), the goal of this text is not to argue which tools work best but to demonstrate basic methods that apply to whichever system you choose. The tool is less important than getting to the music making as quickly as possible. Choose a method that makes the most sense for you and your singers and use it in a logical, sequential, and consistent way. Ensure that your singers use the tool with expression. Most important, they should always be making music.

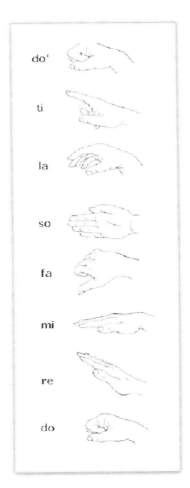

In combination with the solfa, using hand signs is a great tool for working on choral ear training and teaching melodies to singers once they are fluent with the names of their corresponding sounds. An added benefit of the hand signs is that they are a kinesthetic response to something that is heard. Singers can "feel" the contour of melody, the up-and-down motion of notes, when they show the hand signs higher and lower in coordination with the movement of the tones.

8

Important: Avoid writing the solfege names or abbreviations for them under the staff notation. Doing so encourages the singers to read below the staff rather than the music notation *on* the staff. It will be very easy for your singers to remember and perform the names since you will only teach one, two, or three, at most, at a time.

RHYTHM TOOLS

One of the most common tools for reading and performing rhythm are the names adopted by Kodály shown here. These work well for singers of all ages. Consider using counting, based on the sophistication and age of your singers.

<table>
<tr><td>ta</td><td>ta</td><td>ti - ti</td><td>ta</td><td>ti-ri - ti - ri - ti - ti - ri - ti-ri - ti</td><td>ta</td><td>taa</td><td>syn-co - pa</td><td>tai - ti</td><td>tim-ri ri-tim</td><td>taaaa</td></tr>
<tr><td>1</td><td>2</td><td>3 and</td><td>4</td><td>1 e and a 2 and a 3 e and 4</td><td></td><td>1</td><td>3 and and</td><td>1 and</td><td>3 a 4 e</td><td>1</td></tr>
</table>

There are other systems of rhythmic reading, including *takadimi* and the use of common words that correspond to rhythms. I have a colleague who uses states' names for rhythm reading: Maine for the quarter note; Utah for two eighth notes; Delaware for triplets; Mississippi for four sixteenth notes; Michigan for two sixteenth notes with an eighth note; and so on. More information on this can be found in many textbooks and online.

SUGGESTED ORDER OF PRESENTATION

I outline below a sample order for presenting melodic and rhythmic elements, but your choral repertoire determines which elements to teach and in what order. Rearrange the lessons in this book as you need them, as they occur in your repertoire. Remember, as in language learning and teaching, you will be most successful beginning with what students already know and then moving toward more complex concepts and contexts. This process will lead to better mastery and understanding for your singers. Avoid trying to do too much too quickly. When you begin teaching the concepts, each music reading procedure should be short (no more than four to six minutes), since you must balance the teaching process with practicing repertoire for upcoming choral performances.

Note: The musical material the singers will be performing will, of course, contain much more complex material then they are able to read. A mixture of rote and conscious reading is perfect in the rehearsals. As your singers progress with their reading skills, rote teaching will occur less and less.

Sample Order of Melodic Elements

The concepts shown with asterisks can be rearranged in the sequence according to the repertoire you have chosen.

drm
drm s*
drmfs*
drm sl (introduces the pentatonic scale)
drmf*
drm sl d'
s This should be s,l, drm sl d' t, drm sl d'
ti

Bring in other tones, including chromatic tones, as they occur in your repertoire, and as needed.

Sample Order of Rhythmic Elements

Bring in other rhythms as they occur in your scores, and as needed.

BUILDING A FOUNDATION

FOLK SONGS TO BUILD FOUNDATION

SIMPLE FOLK SONGS PROVIDE a great foundation for music reading. Once your students know the songs and can sing them well and in tune (without the aid of a conductor or piano), you can use the songs as teaching tools. Many of these folk songs can also be sung in canon. Singing canons and rounds builds part-singing skills, strengthens in-tune singing, and is great for choral performance as well.

At all levels of education, adapt the lesson to the skillset of your singers. With younger or beginner singers, perform the songs with the words. More advanced singers may be able to use neutral syllables as you would do in vocal warm-ups. Don't worry about the solfa when you begin to teach the exercises. That will come later. Some singers may already come to you with the foundation they need, having learned these skills from a general music class. Great! Move right on to excerpting from folk songs and choral scores to reinforce what they know, teach them the new concepts, and quickly move them to sight-reading. Remember, always meet the singers where they are and with what they already know, and then show them something new.

The following songs feature, respectively, the sequences mrd, drm s, and drm sl (verse only), d' (refrain):

Hot Cross Buns

Let Us Chase the Squirrel

D Major

American Traditional

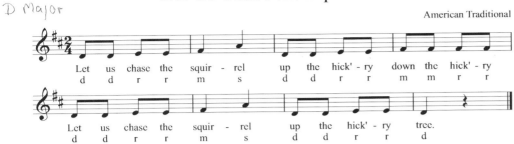

Let us chase the squir - rel up the hick' - ry down the hick' - ry
d   d   r   r   m   s   d   d   r   r   m   m   r   r

Let us chase the squir - rel up the hick' - ry tree.
d   d   r   r   m   s   d   d   r   r   d

Li'l Liza Jane

D Major

American Traditional

Come my love and go with me, Li'l Li - za Jane. Come my love and go with me, Li'l Li - za
m   m   r   d   m   s   s   l   s   m   s   m   m   r   d   m   s   s   m   m   r

Jane. Oh, E - li - za, Li'l Li - za Jane! Oh, E - li - za, Li'l Li - za Jane!
d   d'   s   l   s   l   s   m   s   d'   s   l   s   m   m   r   d

Begin the canon, or round, according to the numbers above the staff. The first group begins, and when they arrive at 2, the second group enters, and so on. The following songs feature, respectively, the sequences l,, s,, and l pentatonic; f; and t,:

Canoe Song

G Major

Canadian Traditional

My   pad - dle's   keen   and   bright,   fla - shing   with   sil - ver,
m   m   r   d   l,   l,   d   d   r   m   l

touched   by   the   pale   moon - light,   dip   dip   and   swing.
m   m   r   d   l,   l,   l,   l,   s,   l,

Alleluia Round

F Major

Traditional

Al - le - lu - ia, al - le - lu - ia, al - le - lu - ia, sing   a - men.
s   f   m   d   r   r   m   f   s   f   m   r   d   r   d

Chairs to Mend

White Sand and Gray Sand

Come, Let's Dance

Additional resources for folk song materials can be found in the following collections and similar ones:

150 American Folk Songs: To Sing, Read and Play
Peter Erdei
Boosey & Hawkes

Sail Away: 155 American Folk Songs to Sing, Read and Play
Eleanor Locke
Boosey & Hawkes

150 Rounds for Singing and Teaching
Edward Bolkavac and Judith Johnson
Boosey & Hawkes

Folksongs, Singing Games, and Play Parties for Kids of All Ages
My Little Rooster (vol. 1)
Bought Me a Cat (vol. 2)
John, the Rabbit (vol. 3)
The Little Black Bull (vol. 4)
Jill Trinka
Gia Publications

UTILIZING VOCALISES TO BUILD FOUNDATION

As a choral director, you know many standard vocal warm-ups that can be used to build foundations for music literacy. Try singing them on neutral syllables while moving up and down by half steps. Once the singers know the vocalises well, you will be able to draw on them to teach the solfa names and rhythm syllable or counting.

If your singers already know the solfa for the full major diatonic scale, they should sing the following warm-ups with the solfa names. If they do not know the names, then they should either sing a neutral syllable or wait to sing the exercises until they know the names (in the meantime, they can vocalize on neutral syllables). Use them with a d-s drone, either played on the piano at the beginning of each measure or sung by two sections of the chorus who sustain the perfect fifth drone by humming or using a neutral syllable. The drone exercise helps improve intonation by developing good in-tune hearing and singing.

Full Scale

This exercise can be sung in canon up to eight parts beginning after one beat. It also works well beginning after two beats.

Two-Part Complete Major Scale

ADDITIONAL CONCEPTS YOUR SINGERS SHOULD KNOW

Your students must also know five key concepts that will be crucial to their understanding of music notation. Mastery of the following ideas is basic to musical literacy. Spread this instruction out over many rehearsals to avoid overwhelming your singers. Move forward with new information only as fast as they are able to master the concepts. I recommend only about four to six minutes per rehearsal for this type of instruction, although older and more experienced singers may be able to sustain concentration in longer lessons.

1. Beat versus Rhythm

Pulse

If you ask beginning musicians what they like about a song, they often say they like the beat without really knowing what that means. The beat is actually the least interesting part of a composition. What the musicians probably mean is that they like the rhythm. The simplest way to understand the difference between the two is to think of the rhythm as the way the words sound, the way they move, and the beat as the silent, steady pulse of the music.

2. High/Low verses Loud/Soft

People will often say, "Turn down that music! It's too high!" when they mean the music is too loud. In the English language, the terms "loud" and "soft" can often be confused with high and low. This confusion is even more common in younger singers. When your singers have mastery of high versus low, they will be able to accurately describe new melodic tones in relation to the tones they already know. For example, when la is introduced they will be able to identify and describe it as the tone that is just higher than so.

3. Fast versus Slow

The difference between fast and slow will be self-explanatory for older singers but will have to be explained to very young singers. Singers of all skill levels must understand the distinction.

4. The Staff

Your singers must learn the basic mechanics of the staff. They must understand that the staff has five lines and four spaces, and the first line and first space are on the bottom and above them are the second line and space, and so on. They must also know what a note looks like when it is on a line or in a space, and the difference between moving by a step and moving by a skip. The music moves by a step when it moves from a line to the very next space or a space to the very next line and moves by a skip when it moves from line to line or space to space. This understanding becomes crucial when you begin to relate the staff to the piano keyboard.

5. The Piano Keyboard

Your singers should know that the keyboard is made up of black and white keys and that each key has a name. It is helpful to teach singers where C is on the keyboard by explaining that it is always the white key just before the set of two black keys. They should also learn that the white keys follow the musical alphabet. Try singing "A B C D E F . . . A B C D E F G . . ." and so on to the alphabet song we all learned as children. It works!

Singers must also understand the difference between a whole and a half step. Moving from one key to the next with no other key in between is called a half step. Moving from one key to another with one key in between is a whole step. Eventually you will relate this to the full major scale so that the singers understand where the whole and half steps are in relationship to the corresponding solfa. When the singers have an understanding of the piano keyboard, introducing sharps and flats also becomes easier since they have a visual representation of half steps and better understand higher and lower.

LESSON 1
TEACHING DO-RE-MI

BEGINNING WITH DRM IS COMMON for older beginners. With very young singers, many teachers begin melodic study with sm, since those sounds make up much of the repertoire they sing at that age and experience. These three tones are quite common in choral music, and chances are they are already in the music you have selected to perform, which is why starting with drm makes sense. Consider finding compositions that feature drm prevalently and programming it at the beginning of the year. Strategic planning and programming of the selection of music make the teaching of melodic and rhythmic elements much easier.

The teaching process for making drm a fluent part of your singers' knowledge should be logical and sequential. Ask your singers leading questions that guide them to analyze what they hear. The logic of the following teaching procedure allows you to add additional tones as the experience of your singers progresses. I use one of the previous warm-ups to demonstrate this lesson here; however, you should use any drm melody that your singers know well.

Two Part Vocal Warm-up

PROCEDURE

   A. Ask your singers to listen as you sing the top part on [lu] (International Alphabet for loo) and then tell you how many different sounds they hear. (They should answer that there are three.)

B. Ask them to listen again and this time notice how the sounds move, that is, describe the contour of the melody. (They should explain that they move up and down, higher and lower.)

C. Ask your singers to listen another time, and this time tell if the sounds are close together or far apart. With younger or more inexperienced singers, playing the top part on a tone ladder will provide a helpful visual clue. (They should say the sounds are close to each other.)

D. You then ask, "If the sounds are close to each other, then are they a step apart or a skip apart?" (Step apart: remember, they learned this terminology through the work you led them through in the introduction of the mechanics of the staff.)

E. Now draw the first note on the staff in the first space.

F. Ask your singers, "Does the next sound move up or down?" (Up.) "Where on the staff, then, if it's a step higher, should we place the second sound?" (Second line.) Add the second note to the staff.

G. Repeat the process for the third note. Make sure you repeat the singing of the top part on [lu] as needed to allow the singers to discover and tell the correct answer.

H. Instruct them to sing the top part on [lu] as you add the rest of the notes to the staff.

I. Ask your singers to sing again on [lu] and watch the staff to make sure all the notes are correct.

J. Now, tell them the names of the notes. "These three sounds that are a step apart from each other are called d, r, and m. They sound like this and have these hand signs." Demonstrate the correct way to sing the melody with solfa and hand signs. When you use the hand signs, make sure that you start d low and then raise your hand for r and m so that your singers can see and feel the relative contours of the melody. **Reminder:** Never write the solfege names or abbreviations underneath the staff notation. If you do, the singers will read the names instead of the notes on the staff. Remember, the goal of this instruction is to teach singers how to read music notation on the staff. And always demonstrate with good musical expression!

K. They should now sing the melody with the solfa names and hand signs as you or another singer points to the staff to ensure all are reading and following the notes on the staff. Repeat this a few times with different student leaders pointing to the staff in order to practice and reinforce d, r, and m.

This exercise will probably take a bit of time and is more than enough for one rehearsal. It is an important step, however, because it shows your singers *how* to learn; they learn that they can listen to a melody and begin to analyze what they are hearing on the basis of what they already know. Remember, they have all the information to answer your questions correctly since you taught it to them earlier. If they cannot answer your questions, refer to the section "Additional Concepts Your Singers Should Know" in the preceding chapter ("Building a Foundation").

Visit the companion website to view a video of this lesson.

You can reinforce the exercise by immediately applying it to the ensemble's repertoire. For example, you can excerpt and sing with solfa and hand signs a pattern from a piece the singers are currently practicing and ask them, "What composition does this come from?" before proceeding with rehearsal.

REINFORCEMENT THROUGH SIGHT-SINGING

The following reinforcement activity practices drm by echo-singing patterns from the conductor, and by sight-singing a new melody excerpted from the ending of the two-part arrangement of "Celtic Cradle Song." The echo-singing will focus on tuning up the major third leap from d to m that occurs in the choral arrangement.

Important: Sight-singing for beginners is always easier when the tuning up activity is done while they perform from *staff notation*. Using the tone ladder with only solfege letters does not provide enough information for the singers to read something new well. Use staff notation. They will have greater success.

Celtic Cradle Song

Arranged by Robert I. High

Traditional Irish Song

Prepare the board with the following melodic patterns before the choristers arrive for rehearsal:

Celtic Cradle Song Warm-up exercises

And

Celtic Cradle Song, sight reading

Important: It is crucial that the excerpt from the score you are addressing appears on the board in the same way it appears to the singers in their scores.

21

Doing so creates a much easier transition from the work you do as a group from the board notation to each singer's individual reading in the score. This is especially true for work with younger beginners.

PROCEDURE

A. As part of your warm-up that develops the ear, sing a single pattern from the board, A through G, and ask the choristers to echo it back with solfa and hand signs. Perform this activity at the ability level of your singers. If they are beginners, sing the patterns with solfa and hand signs in the order you have them on the board. If your singers are more advanced, sing the patterns in random order on [lu] and ask them to identify which pattern you sang. Call on one singer to give the answer. If that singer is incorrect, sing the pattern again and give the singer a second chance to find the correct answer. You can then ask that singer to come up to the board and point to the entire melodic pattern as the entire chorus performs it with solfa and hand signs. If your singers are even more advanced, after the echo-singing drill, ask them to sing all the patterns with solfa and hand signs without stopping as you (or a chorister) point to the notation on the board.

B. Drawing the singers' attention to the excerpt of "Celtic Cradle Song" on the board, say to the singers, "I will sing this new pattern on [lu]. You should show the hand signs and think the solfa as you follow along." It will be helpful to the beginner singers if you show the hand signs, too, underneath the staff notation in order to help guide their reading on the staff. This type of guidance is important since they are new at reading notes on the staff. If your singers are more advanced you should ask them to sing the melody right away as you point to each note. As they perform the exercise, make sure that you are watching them to assess their ability to show the correct hand signs as they read the staff notation.

C. Now say, "Good. This time as I point (or show the hand signs under each note), show the hand signs and sing the solfa."

D. Practice this new skill by repeating the reading while smaller groups, quartets, trios, duets, and soloists perform. If someone is doing particularly well, ask that singer to come forward to point to the notation on the board to lead the ensemble's reading.

E. "Now turn to 'Celtic Cradle Song' and look at the last two pages. Who can find the pattern we have just read on the board and tell me where on these two pages it begins?" (It begins on the last note of page 6.)

F. "Now it's your turn to be your own leader. Sing the same solfa names that we just practiced as you point to the notes and read in your own score. When you get to the last page, make sure you sing the notes for the second staff from the top." Repeat this step as needed as you help singers who are having difficulty following the score.

G. "Now try singing the words from your score as you follow and point to the notes on the staff."

H. Continue with the rest of your rehearsal.

Any of these activities can be done with any choral composition that has a strong drm melodic pattern in it. Substitute your own repertoire in any of these activities. It takes only a little effort to find them.

For example, another good option to teach or practice drm is the choral arrangement of "Three French Folk Songs." The melodic form of each verse is AABA. Each A phrase contains only the tones drm.

Three French Folk Songs

G.E. and various sources

GEOFFREY EDWARDS
Based on the harmonizations of GABRIEL PIERNÉ

dim.
feu.

O-pen wide the win - dow, let the moon-light in.
Ou-vre moi ta por - te, pour l'a-mour de Dieu.

Visit the companion website to download additional sight-singing exercises.

SUGGESTED COMPOSITIONS

"May Song" (first two phrases of each verse)
Franz Schubert
Edited by Doreen Rao
Two-part treble
Boosey & Hawkes
OCTB6578

"Beside Thy Cradle Here I Stand" (first phrase)
Johann Sebastian Bach
Novello

"I've Got Shoes" (measures 4–8)
Traditional spiritual
Arranged by Rollo A. Dillworth
Hal Leonard Corporation
08551500

LESSON 2
TEACHING THE TREBLE CLEF AND LETTER NAMES

AN IMPORTANT PART of learning solfa is understanding that d is moveable and can be placed anywhere on the staff. Even though it is on different places on the staff, the pitches still sound the same relative to each other. The melody does not change; it merely sounds higher or lower.

PROCEDURE

During the end of vocal warm-ups at your next rehearsal, sing the two-part exercise used in lesson 1 to teach drm, and end in G major. Ask your singers to perform the top part with solfa and hand signs.

A. Draw the note head for d on the second line and ask your singers, "Where is d today?" (Second line.)
B. Ask, "If r is a step higher, where does it go on the staff?" (Second space.) Draw the note r on the staff.
C. "If m is a step higher, than r, where does it go on the staff?" (Third line.) Draw the note m on the staff.

Note: Consider drawing a "do clef" on the staff by adding d on the line or space where do is in the lesson, in this case on the second line.

D. Ask them to sing the entire melody with solfa and hand signs, as you draw the rest of the song on the staff.

E. Ask the singers to perform it again as you point to the staff notation to make sure they are reading and following the staff notation.

F. Add a treble clef to the beginning of the staff and ask if anyone knows the name of the new symbol. (Treble or G clef.)

G. "Musicians have other names for these sounds. The treble clef is also known as the G clef since it shows us where G is on the staff. Notice how the lower part of the clef circles around the second line. This circle shows you where G is on the staff, on the second line. The note a step higher is the note A. And the note a step higher than A is B. Now that we have the treble clef, we can sing the letter names." You then demonstrate how to sing the letter names without hand signs, since the signs are specific to the solfa names.

H. Ask the students to sing the letter names. Repeat several times, in smaller groups and solos, to practice this new concept. End by asking everyone to sing the letter names.

I. Finally, ask everyone to sing solfa with hand signs.

During the same rehearsal, try to create a transition to your repertoire so your singers can immediately apply what they just learned.

For example, consider Franz Schubert's "May Song":

May Song

PROCEDURE

Write the following on the board before your singers arrive at rehearsal, taking care to space the melody to approximate Schubert's rhythm:

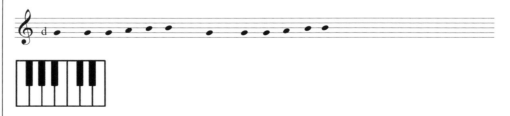

A. Ask your singers if they can still sing d from the previous exercise, and then have everyone sing d with the hand sign.

B. Ask them to perform "May Song" with solfa and hand signs as you point to the melody in the correct rhythm.

C. Ask them to sing the melody with letter names while viewing, in turn:
   1. The staff notation
   2. A keyboard graphic; ask, "What kind of steps are between d and r? What about between r and m?" (Whole steps.)

D. Ask your singers to turn to the score and sing the first two phrases with solfa and hand signs.

E. Repeat the exercise with letter names.

F. Ask them to sing the passage with words, and continue the rehearsal.

Once the students have been introduced to drm, you should develop their knowledge through reinforcement activities. For suggestions, see the appendix.

With a bit of analysis and planning, it is easy to teach beginners music reading. With these types of activities we can all feel better about our leadership when we impart real musical skills to our musicians, as opposed to teaching the repertoire solely by rote or by "banging out" the parts on the piano.

Note: Notice that I have not presented rhythm yet. For beginners, it is best to concentrate on one element at a time. At this point, it is more important the students understand and perform drm, since these three tones provide the entire foundation for the melodic discovery process. For now, you can point at the melodic notation in the rhythm that comes from the score, thereby teaching the rhythm by rote. If your singers are older and more experienced, you can certainly add rhythm if your rehearsal time allows. Refer to the lessons dealing with rhythm when your singers are ready.

27

LESSON 3A
TEACHING THE QUARTER NOTE WITH TWO EIGHTH NOTES

CHOOSE A PIECE OF MUSIC, folk song, or choral composition that has a quarter note followed by two eighth notes together in one beat. If you want to teach quarter rest at the same time, skip ahead to Lesson 3B. Remember that it is your repertoire that tells you what to teach and in what sequence.

For teaching the quarter note with two eighth notes, consider a composition similar to "Mrs. Jenny Wren." It is a good choice since its melody contains only quarter notes and eighth notes, making it a useful tool for teaching rhythmic reading. The song is also a wonderful unison composition for younger singers.

Mrs. Jenny Wren

Rodney Bennett

Arthur Baynon

PROCEDURE

A. Ask half of the singers to pat the beat while listening to the other half sing the words and clap the rhythm of the first phrase of "Mrs. Jenny Wren."

B. Switch the groups and ask them to repeat the exercise.

C. Explain to your singers: "Sometimes we hear one sound on a beat, and sometimes we hear something different on one beat. When it's different, how many sounds do you hear?" Repeat the exercise so they can discover two sounds on one beat. If your singers are very young, this is a good place to stop and move on to another activity. You can finish the rest of the procedure at the next rehearsal. If they are older, continue with the following steps in the same rehearsal.

D. The next step—moving from the ear to the eye: before the singers come to rehearsal, write the beats of the song on the board. For example, "Mrs. Jenny Wren":

— — — — — — — — — — — — — — — — —

1. "Sing the words and clap the rhythm as I point to the beats, and then tell me how many sounds you hear on these beats." (They will reply that there are two sounds for the first two beat, one sound for the third beat, and two sounds for the fourth beat. Draw lines to represent the sounds on the beats.)

‖ ‖ | ‖ — — — — — — — — — — — —

2. Continue until the whole phrase has been completed.

E. Point to the first two beats and say, "Since these two sounds happen on the same beat, we join them together by connecting them with a line known as a beam."

 etc...

F. Teaching singers to name the rhythms:
1. Choose the system of rhythm counting or syllables you want to use.
   a. With younger singers, try syllables.
      i. "Musicians call two sounds on one beat 'ti ti' and one sound on a beat 'ta.'"
      ii. You sing and clap the phrase with the syllables.
      iii. Your singers perform the phrase with the syllables as they sing the melody.
      iv. Repeat and reinforce with smaller groups and solos.

29

b. With older singers, you can use counting.
   i. "Let's draw bar lines after each fourth beat. Now we can sing and count the beat numbers in groups of four." At this time, you can also introduce time signature.
   ii. You then sing the phrase with counting, "One-and two-and three four-and, etc."

2. Finish the instruction by asking everyone to clap and sing the rhythm names or by counting from the board.

3. Finally, ask the singers to turn to their scores of "Mrs. Jenny Wren" and perform the same music with rhythm names or with counting as they point to the rhythm on the staff.

G. Ask the singers to sing the words from their scores as they point to the staff notation.

Again, it may take a little more time initially to introduce rhythm the first time you teach it to your ensemble. Now that your singers have a foundation to analyze what they are hearing, they will pick up additional rhythms faster.

The same type of activities for teaching the quarter note with two eighth notes can be accomplished by using other compositions that may be in your repertoire. For example, "Hopi, Hop" from "Deux Poules Françaises" is an effective choice. Notice how the melody contains only the rhythms of the quarter note with two eighth notes.

Deux Poules Françaises
Hopi, Hop

French children's song
arr. Sheila Donahue

la poul' a bat-tu le coq,   le ca-nard va au mar - ché

If your singers already know the words and melody to the song, you should consider using it as a practice activity. Perhaps they can sight-read the simple rhythms from notation written on the board in front of the choral room. You can even make four rhythm cards, mixed up, on which you write one beat of rhythm from measures 5 and 6. Ask the choristers to sing the song and then arrange the cards in the correct order. Then ask them to sing the song with counting, or rhythm names. End the activity by asking them to sing the words. For other reinforcement ideas, refer to the appendix.

REMINDER

Whenever working on musical elements of rhythm and melody, after the singers perform with counting, rhythm names, letter names, or solfa, be sure to perform the music with the words. The lessons will have a wonderful sense of music making whenever you return back to what the composer originally wrote. And when you as teacher demonstrate the solfege and rhythm counting make sure you do so with the artistic expression that is called for by the music. Always be musical. The singers will enjoy the process of learning music reading much more when they experience the instruction in this musical way.

SUGGESTED COMPOSITIONS

"Bashana Haba' Ah" (alto, measures 9–12)
Nurit Hirsch
Edited by Henry Leck
Hal Leonard Corporation
08602199

"Al la Puerta del Cielo" (measures 5–12)
Mexican lullaby
Arranged by Melissa Roth
Two-part treble with piano
Alliance Music Publications
AMP 0624

31

LESSON 3B
TEACHING THE QUARTER NOTE WITH QUARTER REST AND TWO EIGHTH NOTES

THIS LESSON DIFFERS from the previous one by adding the quarter rest. The new key concept is that your singers hear one beat that has no sound on it. The folk song "Hot Cross Buns" is a good choice. However, if you have a phrase in your choral music that has a quarter note, quarter rest, and two eighth notes, you can excerpt and use that phrase.

PROCEDURE

A. "Sing 'Hot Cross Buns' with the words and tap the beat on your laps."

B. "Sopranos sing the words as the altos listen and pat the beat. As you do this, altos, sometimes you will hear one sound on a beat, and some beats that have a different number of sounds on them. When it's different, how many sounds do you hear on the beat?" All perform the activity.

C. "Before you answer, let's give the sopranos a chance to answer my questions. Remember, sopranos, that you will hear one sound on one beat, and beats that have a different number of sounds on them. When it's different from one sound, how many sounds do you hear?" All perform the activity.

D. "One more time, before you answer, everyone pat the beat, and I will sing the words by myself. You will hear one sound on one beat and something different. When it's different, how many sounds are on one beat?" (Two and no sounds.) The repetition of this activity as I have described it in this process gives the singers a chance to double check what they are hearing and allows them to listen more carefully in order to come up with the correct answer.

E. "This time, look at the beats that I have on the board. Sing the words again as I point to the beats. When we're done, tell me how many sounds to draw on each beat: one; two; or none." If this is difficult for them, it will be helpful to have them sing only four beats at a time until all the beats are filled in.

F. Point to the first beat and say, "One sound on one beat is called 'ta'" (or "quarter note," or whatever name is consistent with the rhythm tool you choose to use). Point to the ninth beat and say, "Since these two sounds occur on the same beat, we add a beam at the top of the stems to join them together and call them 'ti-ti.' No sound on one beat is called 'rest.'" (Draw in the symbol for rest.) "Listen as I sing and clap the rhythm names." **Note:** I recommend singing nothing on the rest since it is, after all, a beat that has no sound on it. Some teachers like to have their singers perform "shh" for rest. It is my experience that beginning students do not need to do this. When you get to the rest on the notation, simply pull your hands apart to indicate (silently) *we do not clap for rest.*

G. "Now it's your turn to sing the rhythm names and clap as I point to the board."

H. Practice the new skills with just the sopranos or altos, with smaller groups, with duets, and with soloists performing. End with everyone. Finally, have everyone sing the words of the song.

REINFORCEMENT THROUGH GUIDED SIGHT-READING

Try applying the same teaching technique to a composition similar to "Fum, Fum, Fum." Look for a passage that has quarter notes, two eighth notes, and quarter rests prominent in simple, repetitive phrases.

Fum, Fum, Fum

Spanish Dance Carol
Traditional
Arrangeds by Judy Herrington
and Sara Glick

PROCEDURE

Prepare the board with the following rhythms, or similar ones, before the singers arrive for rehearsal:

Fum, Fum, Fum activity

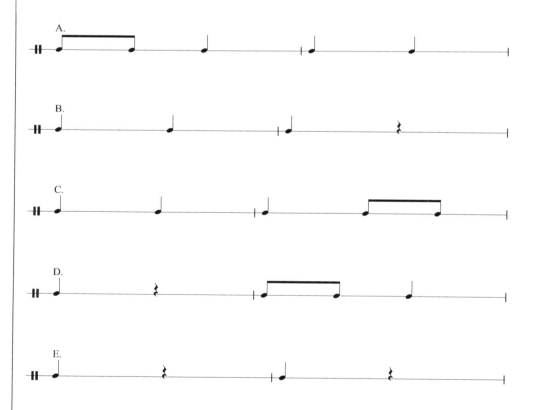

And

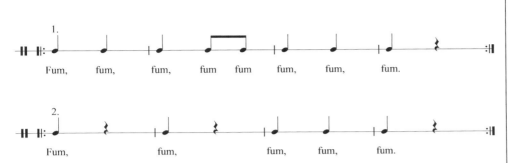

1.
Fum,   fum,   fum,   fum fum fum,   fum,   fum.

2.
Fum,   fum,   fum,   fum,   fum.

A. Warm-up activity:
   1. Say to the singers, "Look at the rhythms, A through E, on the board. I am going to clap one of them. See if you can tell which letter I am clapping." Clap the rhythms in random order. When a singer answers correctly, ask him or her to go to the board to point to the notes as everyone claps and counts that rhythm. Be sure to do this activity at your singers' level. For example, if they are more experienced you can simply clap the rhythms for them to identify. If they are beginners you should clap *and* count the rhythms.
   2. Once the singers can read, clap, and count the rhythms well, you can ask individual singers to choose and clap and count the rhythms for the class to identify. This is an effective way to challenge singers in your ensemble who may have more advanced skills.
B. Reading "Fum, Fum, Fum":
   1. Point to the first rhythm of "Fum, Fum, Fum" on the board. If the singers do not know about the repeat sign, this is a good opportunity to introduce the symbols. Ask the entire group to clap and count the rhythm. Practice the reading by asking smaller groups, half of the singers, trios, duets, and even solos to perform the rhythms. End by asking half the group to clap and count the rhythm as the other half claps and speaks the words. Switch.
   2. Repeat the process with the second rhythm.
   3. Perform both rhythms simultaneously.
      a. All count and clap in two parts.
      b. All clap and speak the words in two parts.
C. Depending on the age and experience of the singers, you might stop here and continue with a different activity. However, if they are older and more experienced, lead them through step B by asking them to read from their scores. **Reminder:** Whenever possible, I recommend the final step of the procedure should be the singers performing the reading from their own scores. This is a crucial step, since our ultimate goal is each individual singer reading from his or her own score.

35

ADDING THE TIME SIGNATURE

In addition to suggested reinforcement activities in the appendix, you can add the time signature during the next rehearsal. Look for patterns in the rhythm that tell the singers that the time signature will be either 2/4 or 4/4.

For example, write the rhythm from a song, or excerpt from a choral composition, similar to "Hot Cross Buns" on the board before the singers arrive for rehearsal.

A. "Let's review "Hot Cross Buns" by singing and clapping the rhythm from the board as I point." It is important that you point to the notation, since beginner singers tend to memorize quickly and often do not read the notation unless guided to do so.

B. "Look at the pattern of rhythms in the first four beats. Does this pattern happen again?" (Yes.) Point to the eighth notes and ask, "How many beats of eighth notes do you see?" (Four. They may respond with eight. If this happens, remind them that eighth notes are two sounds on one beat.)

C. "This composition has rhythm patterns of four beats. So, now we can organize these four beats by placing a bar line after each grouping of four. The space between the bar lines is known as a measure, or bar. How many measures are there in 'Hot Cross Buns'?" (Four.)

D. While drawing the final bar line, say, "And since this is the last bar line, and we are at the end of the song, we write two bar lines to show us that the song is over." Draw two bar lines.

E. At this point you can add the meter. What you draw as the time signature will depend on the age and experience of the singers. With very young ones, it may make more sense to them if you add a 4 over a quarter note and explain, "The number four tells us that there are four beats in the measure. And since quarter note [or 'ta'] is one sound on one beat we will write a quarter note underneath the four." With older singers you can add 4 over 4 and explain that the bottom four stands for the quarter note.

F. "We call the numbers at the beginning of the music a time signature, or meter. It tells us how the rhythm of the song is organized."

G. "Listen as I sing and clap the song while counting in groups of fours."

one two three (four) one two three (four) one and two and three and four and one two three (four)

H. "Everyone sing and clap in fours."

I. Continue the practice with smaller groups, duets, and soloists. Ask individual singers to come to the board to point to the notation to lead the ensemble.

J. Apply meter again by telling the singers to open the score of the next piece you would like to rehearse. Ask them about the time signature they find in the composition. At this point, do not spend much time on the explanation of the meter in the new song. It will probably be enough to have them identify it and continue with the rest of the rehearsal.

37

LESSON 4
COMBINING MELODY AND RHYTHM ON THE STAFF

ULTIMATELY, WE WOULD LIKE OUR SINGERS to read and perform melody and rhythm together. So far, they have done them separately. In a very simple process, you can combine the two.

Consider the first phrase of the soprano part from J. S. Bach's "Beside Thy Cradle Here I Stand," a chorale from his *Christmas Oratorio*. You might program it by having your entire ensemble perform only the melody for your winter concert:

PROCEDURE

A. Begin by reviewing individually what the singers already know: drm and quarter note and eighth notes. They should be able to read and sing this without your help. Write the following on the board before they arrive for rehearsal:

1. Singers sing solfa and show hand signs
2. Singers sing letter names

3. Singers sing the rhythm names or counting from the rhythm notation above the staff

B. Tell your singers: "Rhythm and melody are joined together when written on the staff. All we have to do is bring down the rhythm and attach them as stems to the note heads." At this point, as you add the stems to the note heads, explain to the singers that the stems go up when the note heads are below the third line and down when they are on the third line and above.

C. Now erase the rhythm from above the staff and ask the ensemble to sing from the staff notation with the following, as you or a singer points:
   1. Solfa and hand signs
   2. Letter names
   3. Rhythm names or counting

D. Ask the singers to turn to the score and perform the same as above, only this time from their own printed notation.

E. When you have the opportunity (as in the above composition), introduce the concept of anacrusis: music that starts on beats other than the first beat. Make sure they know that the beat is borrowed from the last measure.

F. Finally, sing the words of the melody, and then move on to the rest of rehearsal.

Visit the companion website to view a video of this lesson.

Note: Make sure to put melody and rhythm together on the staff in similar procedures whenever you have repertoire in which your singers know how to sing both the melody with solfa and rhythm counting (or names).

LESSON 5A
TEACHING SOL

ONCE YOU AND YOUR STUDENTS have a system for listening and analyzing, adding notes to the tone set becomes an easy task. Ask the students leading questions, similar to when you taught drm, and they should be able to uncover most of what they need to know about the new tones.

CHOICES TO MAKE ABOUT THE SEQUENCE OF INSTRUCTION

If your students are younger and your repertoire includes drm s patterns, the next step is adding s.

If your students are older and often encounter drmfs patterns in their music, then f and s together will be your next melodic concept.

Perhaps you will teach drm sl before introducing f. If you choose this approach then you should skip to those lessons found later in this book. Always let your repertoire guide you in the order of the concepts you teach.

INTRODUCING SOL ONLY

Choose your repertoire first. If you've taught your singers "Let Us Chase the Squirrel," it is a good choice. If you have been working on a composition similar to "Sleep My Baby," use it. The repertoire will work as long as s is immediately preceded by m. The singers ultimately will have to discover that the "new sound" is a skip higher than m.

Sleep My Baby
Suo Gan

Welsh Slumber Song
English translation by
M. Ll. DAVIES

Arranged by
ALEC ROWLEY

PROCEDURE

A. Begin the ear-training portion of your rehearsal by tuning up drm with your singers. This can be done either by singing known repertoire with solfa or using a reinforcement activity. Make sure that the melody you choose to use is in, or ends in, the same key in which you sing the drm s song. In this case, the key will be F major.

B. Tell your singers: "I am going to sing for you a song you know that begins on d. Listen carefully and tell me if you hear a tone that is different from d, r, and m." (Sing the song on [lu].)

C. "Did you hear a new sound? Was it higher or lower?" (Higher.)

D. "Raise your hands when you hear me sing the new, higher sound." When they raise their hands, you can assess whether most of them hear it, and hear it in the correct place in the song.

E. "Does it sound a step higher than m or a skip higher?" (A skip higher.) Younger singers will find it easier to answer this question correctly if you provide a visual aid by playing the song with resonator bells on a ladder.

F. Staff notation:

   1. Before the singers come in for rehearsal write the first two phrases of "Sleep My Baby" on the board, omitting s:

2. "If d is on the first space, r is on the second line, m is on the second space, and the new sound is a skip higher than m, where do we write the new sound on the staff?" (Third space.) Draw the note head for s.

G. Naming the new sound:

1. "I will now sing for you the name and show the hand sign of the new sound that is a skip higher than m." Sing the music with solfa and hand signs. Show the signs just below each note on the staff on the board, in order to guide the singers to read the notes on the staff.

2. "Everyone sing with solfa and hand signs." Repeat with smaller groups and solos, and complete the exercise as a group.

3. "Let's now sing letter names."

4. "Now end with solfa and hand signs."

H. Apply to the musical score.

1. "Turn to 'Sleep My Baby,' page 1. Can you still read the score and sing solfa?"

2. "Try reading the letter names from the score."

3. "Sing the words."

I. Continue with the rest of the rehearsal.

With practice and careful thought, you as conductor can teach this concept in a time-efficient manner.

REINFORCEMENT OF SOL THROUGH GUIDED SIGHT-READING FROM STICK NOTATION

CIRCLE 'ROUND THE MOON

Words and Music by
Mark Hierholzer

PROCEDURE

Prepare the board with the following:

Circle 'Round the Moon, stick notation

m s m d d   d m s m d d d   r d m   d   d_____

A. End the warm-up portion of rehearsal by asking your singers to practice the tone set d r m s. Ask them to sing from the tone ladder as you point to simple four-beat patterns. I demonstrate this in the examples below that tune the melodic difficulties found in "Circle 'round the Moon." Remember to lead the singers through this exercise at the level where they will be most successful. If they are younger or very inexperienced, they can echo the patterns after you sing them with solfa. If they are more advanced, they can sing the patterns as you point to them.

Circle 'Round the Moon, melodic tuning up stick notation

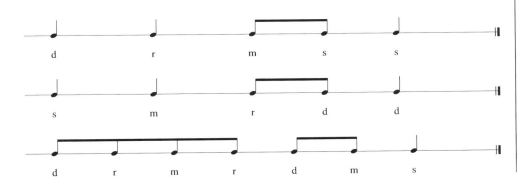

And

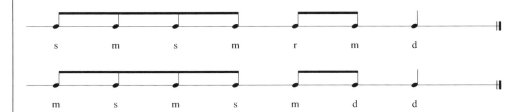

s	m	s	m	r	m	d

m	s	m	s	m	d	d

B. Using the "Circle 'round the Moon" excerpt on the board, ask the choristers to sing with solfa as you point to one measure at a time. You can also try a more advanced method by asking them to hand-sign and inner hear, or audiate, as you point to each measure, and then ask them to sing it back by memory.

C. Ask the singers to inner hear and hand-sign as you point to the melody in all four measures.

D. Ask them to sing the entire pattern with solfa and hand signs as you point.

E. Optional: If you have the time, practice more advanced inner hearing skills. Ask the singers to perform the entire phrase. Each time they do it, tell them to inner hear a different tone or two. For example, first ask them to sing the entire phrase while inner hearing r. The second time, ask them to inner hear d. Repeat for the other tones. For the tone(s) they are audiating, the singers should always "think" or imagine the melodic tone while showing the hand sign.

F. Tell the singers to take out "Circle 'round the Moon" and explain that the first two phrases are exactly what they practiced on the board.

G. Ask them to sing the first two phrases with solfa as they point to each note.

H. Ask the altos to sing solfa as the sopranos sing the words of the song.

I. Switch roles.

J. Ask everyone to sing the words.

K. Continue with the rest of your rehearsal.

 Visit the companion website to view a video of this lesson.

REINFORCEMENT OF SOL BY "WRITING THE MISSING NOTES ON THE STAFF"

Another effective way to practice melody is by asking the singers to complete a well-known melody by writing in omitted notes. This activity can be done in different ways, depending on the age and experience of the singers. If they are very young and inexperienced it should be accomplished with your guidance while everyone completes it together on the board. If the choristers are older and more experienced, they can copy the melody with the missing notes from the board and fill in the notes on their own staff paper. Individuals can then be asked to go up to the board to write in one or two of the missing notes so that all can check their own work. A positive aspect of these types of activities is that they can always be tailored to the level of your unique group of singers.

Select a composition containing drm s that the singers know well. "Kyrie," an arrangement based on the famous tune Dvořák uses in the Largo of his Symphony no. 9, op. 95, is a good example that will work well. Excerpt the first two phrases.

PROCEDURE

A. Prepare the board before the singers arrive for rehearsal:

Kyrie

Arranged by
Ruth Elaine Schram

Based on music by
Antonín Dvořák (1841-1904)

46

Kyrie, Dvorak board preparation

If you are doing this activity with very young singers you can write the melody in staff notation using note heads only and omitting the rhythm:

etc...

B. "Sing the words of first two phrases of 'Kyrie' by memory."

C. Point to the tone ladder and say, "Last rehearsal we learned to sing 'Kyrie' with solfa and hand signs. Who remembers the name of the first note?" (Mi.) "Let's all review the first two phrases with solfa and hand signs." (All sing.)

D. "We're going to play the musical game called 'Fill in the Missing Note.'"

E. Review the staff placement of drm s by saying, as you point to the first note on the staff, "If this is m, and it is on the first line, where will s go on the staff if it is a skip higher?" (Second line.) You, or one of the singers, write the note in the correct place on the staff.

F. Point to the second missing place where the r will go and say, "If r is a step lower than m, where will we write it on the staff?" (The space below the staff.) Draw the note on the staff.

G. "You know that r is on the space below the staff. That means this note on the ledger line must be called what?" (d). "Good. Let's now sing the first two measures with solfa." (All sing.)

H. "Now sing the first staff while inner hearing the melody. Someone volunteer to go up to the board to write in the next missing note." (Singer writes in the missing s.)

I. Continue step H until the missing notes are written in correctly.

J. Ask the choristers to sing the entire song with solfa and hand signs as a volunteer comes forward to point to the notes and leads the ensemble. In all of the steps of this procedure, make sure you are watching the singers to assess how well each chorister is reading the music notation on the board. Try saying, "I am looking for someone who is reading the notes on the staff to be our next leader."

K. "Let's sing the words of 'Kyrie.'"

L. Continue with the rest of the rehearsal by making a transition to your next composition by rehearsing a piece that has a strong drm s pattern. Say to your singers, "Listen as I sing solfa for a pattern that you know from a different composition. Who can tell me the title?" Perhaps you sing the first phrase of "Suo-Gan" or "Circle 'round the Moon." Simply rehearse the next choral piece without a melodic or rhythmic focus. Your young singers have worked hard enough and will do better if you just allow them to sing a piece they know well.

Visit the companion website to download additional sight-reading exercises.

SUGGESTED COMPOSITION

"I'm Gonna Sing When the Spirit Says 'Sing'" (soprano part, measures 3–10)
Traditional spiritual
Arranged by Rochelle Mann and C. Schott Hagler
For three-part voices with piano accompaniment
Colla Voce Music
24-96360

47

LESSON 5B
TEACHING FA AND SOL TOGETHER

IF YOUR CHORISTERS ARE OLDER, have more experience, and if your repertoire includes patterns with drmfs (instead of drm s as in lesson 5A) you can teach f and s in the same lesson.

Begin by choosing your repertoire. I recommend one similar to the "Alleluia Canon," the five-note ascending and descending scale from the known vocalises (drmfsfmrd), "The Piglets Christmas," or the alto part of "Over the Sea to Skye."
Reminder: It is easier to teach new melodic tones and rhythms if the singers know how to sing the composition from which the instruction occurs.

The Piglets' Christmas

Text by Mary Goetze and Nancy Cooper

American Folk Song
Arranged by MARY GOETZE

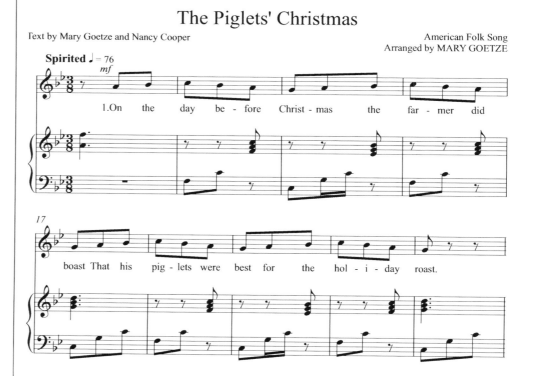

Note: The key signature for "The Piglets' Christmas" indicates B-flat major, even though the singers never sing an E flat and the melody eventually ends on

F (not shown in this excerpt). Therefore, for pedagogical purposes, we can treat the melody as if it is in F major; F = d.

Over the Sea to Skye

Arranged by Joyce Eilers

PROCEDURE

A. Begin the ear-training portion of your rehearsal by tuning up drm with your singers. This can be done either by singing known repertoire with solfa, or by creating a reinforcement activity. Make sure this activity is in, or ends in, the same key in which you sing the drm s composition: F major for "The Piglets' Christmas"; G major for "Over the Sea to Skye."

B. Say: "I am going to sing a song [for example, "The Piglets' Christmas"] you know that begins on m. Listen carefully, and tell me if you hear a tone or tones that are different from d, r, and m." Sing the song on [lu].

C. "Did you hear new sounds? Were they higher or lower?" (Singers should say higher.)

D. "Raise your hands when you hear me sing the new, higher sounds." Sing the song again on [lu].

E. "Does the first new tone sound a step higher than m or a skip higher?" (Step higher.) "Does the second new tone sound a step or skip higher than the other new sound?" (Step higher.) You probably will have to sing the song on [lu] again so your singers can hear the difference and give the correct answer.

F. Staff notation.

1. Have the following already written on the board:

2. "If m is on the second space, and the first new sound is a step higher, where do we write it on the staff?" (Third line.) Bring down the note from above the staff and move it to the correct place for f.

3. "If the next new tone is a step higher than that, where does it go on the staff?" (Third space.) Bring down the note for s.

4. "Sing the song on [lu] as I draw the rest of the notes on the staff."

G. Naming the new sounds.

1. "I will now sing the names and show the hand signs of the new sounds that are higher than m." Sing the melody with solfa and hand signs. Show the signs just below each note on the staff on the board, in order to guide the singers to read the staff notation.

2. "Everyone sing with solfa and hand signs." Repeat with smaller groups and solos, and complete the exercise together as a group.

H. Apply to the musical score.

1. "Turn to 'The Piglets' Christmas,' page 1. Can you still sing solfa as you read from your own part in the score? Make sure you point to the notes on the staff as you read."

2. "Sing the words."

I. Continue with the rest of the rehearsal.

Remember, almost all of the steps for teaching new sounds involve simply asking the singers leading questions based on information they already know. When we as teachers take on the role of coach rather than disseminator of information, and we guide our students through the discovery process, our students will learn better and be more actively engaged in the learning process. And as an added benefit, your singers will be more interested, enthusiastic, and will have fewer behavior problems.

REINFORCEMENT THROUGH GUIDED SIGHT-READING

You are now ready to move fs into other practice and reinforcement exercises using the suggested activities for melodic reinforcement in the appendix.

The next rehearsal might include sight-reading an excerpt from the ensemble's repertoire. "Glory to God," an adaptation of a movement from Giovanni Pergolesi's *Stabat Mater,* allows your singers to practice fs. Vary the sight-reading so your singers read from both stick notation and staff notation.

PROCEDURE

Prepare the board with the tone ladder, keyboard visual, and staves found in this procedure.

    A. End your singers' vocal warm-ups by performing descending five-note scales (sfmrd) from s with:

        1. Neutral syllables

        2. Solfa, ending in the key of G major

52

B. Perform a tone ladder drill from the board in G major. Ask your singers to sing solfa with hand signs as you:

1. Point to various patterns, focusing on melodies similar to the music in the isolated phrases in "Glory to God."
2. Point to patterns as students first inner hear, and then ask them to sing back from memory.

C. Staff notation on the board:

1. Singers perform solfa and hand signs as you point to patterns similar to above.
2. Begin to point to the melody in the rhythm from the first two measures of the treble I part.
3. On the staff with the melodic excerpt: point to staff notation in the rhythm of the composition as all perform solfa and hand signs for the following:

D. Ask your singers: "Now, sing the letter names while looking at the piano keyboard. Are all the steps whole steps? Where is the half step?" (Between m and f, B and C.)

E. Reading from the score
1. "Take out 'Glory to God.' Can you still sing the solfa?" (All sing.)
2. "Now sing from your score with the letter names as you point to the notation."
3. "Sing the words." (All sing words.)

F. Continue with the rest of your rehearsal.

REMINDER: A LITTLE AT A TIME

Notice that we are not working with complete compositions, or even large sections with many measures. In the previous strategy, working with "Glory to God," we extracted only two measures of the score. Not one word was mentioned to the singers about the rhythm. The singers learned the rhythm for "Glory to God" by rote when you pointed to the notes of the phrase on the tone ladder and staff. They can learn syncopation later, along with the eighth note and two sixteenth notes.

The idea of this approach is to use precious rehearsal time to teach music reading without sacrificing mastery of the repertoire that the singers have to learn for upcoming concerts. If we work on reading a little at a time and work it into our rehearsals in a logical and sequential way, then our singers will gain valuable reading skills. Furthermore, once they gain even a few of the skills, you, as a conductor, will discover that you can call on their new knowledge to rehearse and teach other compositions more effectively.

SUGGESTED COMPOSITIONS

"Gloria Deo!" (measures 6–13)
Mary Lynn Lightfoot
Two-part chorus and piano
Heritage Music Press
15/1113

"Across the Western Ocean," no. 3 of *Five Sea Chanties*
(soprano, measures 3–10)
Arranged by Celius Dougherty and Emily Crocker
G. Schirmer
50485803

53

PAUSE AND REMINDERS
INTRODUCING MELODIC TONES AND RHYTHMS

MELODIC PROCESS REVIEW

TEACH BY MOVING FROM what your singers already know. Progress from the ear, what the singer hears, to the eye, the visual representation on the staff of the new note(s) along with the solfa and hand sign(s). Ask the singers leading questions so that they learn by the process of discovery. Continue in the same manner according to the suggested sequence of melodic tones provided earlier in this text. Remember that your own musical repertoire will ultimately decide the order in which you introduce the new concepts.

Often in the melodic process we warm up the singers' ear with an activity that reviews the tones they already know. When you then ask them if they hear a sound that is different or new, and they cannot, then you should not move forward. They are letting you know they need more reinforcement on the tones they know. Refer to the appendix for suggested activities that will help reinforce known melodic tone sets.

As you introduce the new tones, always compare them to the tones the singers already know. For example, once the students know drmfs and you decide to add l, then l should be compared to s, that it is a step higher. And once you add it to staff notation, try singing the tone set with letter names while viewing a piano keyboard visual so they can see that it is a whole step above s.

When you decide to teach l, the students should understand that it is a skip lower than d.

Once you introduce ti (t,), make sure they learn that it is a half step lower than d, through staff notation and keyboard visuals.

Avoid writing solfege names or their abbreviations under staff notation. We should expect the students to become fluent in reading the names from the notation without this crutch.

Use the keyboard visual to begin to teach intervals. For example, once the singers know drm s they should be able to compare and count the number of half steps between d and m and between s and m. Teach them that d to m is a major third (four half steps) and that m to s is a minor third (three half steps) since it is a smaller interval.

INTRODUCING RHYTHMS OVERVIEW

The process of learning quarter note and two eighth notes requires the singers to hear that there are one and two sounds that occurred on one beat. Many other rhythms work similarly. For example, the singers should be able to hear and define the following as:

Rhythms That Occur on One Beat

Four even sounds on one beat.

Three sounds on one beat with a slow sound at the beginning and two fast sounds at the end.

Three sounds on one beat with two fast sounds at the beginning and a slow sound at the end.

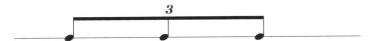

Three even sounds on one beat.

Two uneven sounds on one beat with the faster one at the end.

Two uneven sounds on one beat with the faster one at the beginning.

Using the rhythmic teaching segment for quarter note and two eighth notes in lesson 3A as a model, create your own strategies that lead your singers to the understanding of these rhythms.

55

Rhythms That Occur over Two Beats

One sound that lasts for two beats. Singers can also understand this rhythm by introducing "tie": a half note equals two quarter notes tied together.

Two uneven sounds over two beats with the faster one at the end. You can also teach this rhythm more accurately by having the singers clap an eighth note ostinato, a repeating rhythmic or melodic pattern, that teaches them the first sound lasts for three eighth notes and the last sound lasts for one eighth note.

Two uneven sounds over two beats with the faster one at the beginning. Use an ostinato as above.

Three uneven sounds over two beats that are "short, long ___, short." Using an eighth note ostinato as above will fine-tune the singers' knowledge that the first sound lasts for one eighth note, the second for two eighth notes, and the third for one eighth note.

Keep in mind that the order of presentation of these new rhythms will be determined by need. Your ensemble's repertoire will be the deciding factor. Come up with your own strategies through your own creative and logical pedagogy.

Reminder: Make sure that you combine rhythm and melody during your practice and reinforcement activities for both melodic and rhythmic concepts. The ultimate goal is for the singers to learn to read both together. Add known rhythms to known melodies and ask the singers to perform both the rhythm names, or counting, and the solfa as they view the notation.

LESSON 6
TEACHING THE HALF NOTE

A New Year Carol

Words Anon.

Music by
Benjamin Britten

Quietly

1. Here we bring new wa – ter from the well____ so clear,

For to wor – ship God with this hap – py New Year.

PROCEDURE

A. Tell your singers: "Sing the first two phrases of 'A New Year Carol' from memory while patting the beat on your laps."

B. "Sometimes you will hear one sound on a beat, a quarter note [or ta], and sometimes you will hear two sounds on a beat, two eighth notes [or ti-ti]. You may even hear no sound on a beat, rest. Listen this time as I sing and you pat the beat. Do you hear something different?" (Your singers should say they hear a longer sound.)

C. "Pat the beat again. For how many beats does the longer sound last?" (Two beats.)

D. "On the board, I drew the beats and some of the rhythms for 'A New Year Carol.' Sing the words as I point to the board, then tell me which beats have our new rhythm, the one sound that lasts for two beats." (The last two quarter notes on each line.)

E. "Musicians can join these two quarter notes together in order to make them one sound that last for two beats. We tie them together like this." Add ties on the board.

F. "And we have another way to write the same thing." Erase the last quarter of each line and draw the open note head on the other one, creating a half note. "This is called a half note [or ta-a]."

G. "Listen as I clap and count (or say rhythm names)." Clap and count the rhythm, holding your hands together for two beats to clap the half note. **Note:** If you choose rhythm counting as the tool for your singers, you should insert a time signature at the beginning of the above notation and draw bar lines in the appropriate places.

H. "Sing and clap the rhythm as I point to the board." Practice this with smaller groups, finally ending with everyone performing.

I. "Take out 'A New Year Carol.' Can you sing and clap the rhythm while reading your own score?" Everyone sings and claps together.

J. "Now, sing the words from your scores as you point to the rhythm on the staff."

 Visit the companion website to view a video of this lesson.

REINFORCEMENT THROUGH GUIDED SIGHT-READING

Find another composition, or a different phrase in the piece from which you introduced the half note, and excerpt a phrase for the singers to sight-read. A composition similar to "Kokoleoko" works well. For this activity, use the top vocal part that begins in measure 49. This composition is a good choice to introduce the half note.

Kokoleoko

Liberian Folk Song
Additional Words and Music by
Mary Donnelly (ASCAP)
Arranged by George L.O. Strid (ASCAP)

PROCEDURE

A. Write the following rhythm and words from the top part on the board before the singers arrive for rehearsal:

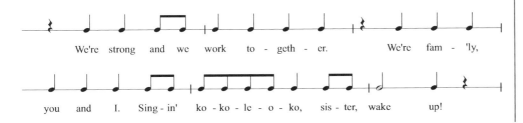

B. Practice the rhythms that the singers already know through an echo clapping activity. At this point, the rhythms will include quarter, eighth, and half notes. Include the quarter rest if you have already introduced it. If the singers are beginners, you should begin by saying the rhythm names (or counting) as you clap. The choristers say the rhythms back as they clap. When your singers become more advanced, you can begin as above and then move toward only clapping the rhythms as the choristers echo them back with counting and clapping. If there are advanced singers in your ensemble, give them a challenge by asking them to individually lead the class in an echo activity. They will be more successful in improvising their own rhythms after they have seen you model the exercise many, many times.

C. Draw their attention to the board and say, "Now try reading this rhythm as you clap and count."

D. Practice the reading by repeating it with everyone, then smaller groups, working your way down to solo performances.

E. Now put the words with the rhythm by saying, "Let's have this side of the chorus clap and say the rhythm names as the other half claps and reads the words underneath." Repeat this as needed.

F. "Good. Let's switch who says the rhythm names and who reads the words."

G. "Now everyone clap the rhythm as you read the words."

H. "Turn to 'Kokoleoko,' page eight. Who can tell everyone in which measure and part you find the rhythm we just learned from the board?" (Part 1, measure 49.) **Note:** I often ask my choristers to find the excerpt in their scores by themselves. This encourages them to look, analyze, and recognize the musical pattern I want them to read."

I. "Now clap the rhythm and read the words from your own scores."

J. Since the focus of this Lesson is to sight-read the rhythm, you are now able to teach the melody by rote. Be careful that you do not ask beginning, younger singers to spend too much time in this type of concentrated activity. Most likely, asking them to read the melody with solfa or letter name will be too much. Teach the melody by rote and move on with your rehearsal.

SUGGESTED COMPOSITIONS

"Four Seasons of Haiku, Autumn Fun" (measures 5–12)
Jerry Estes
For two-part voices, piano, and percussion
Alfred Publishing
21181

"Ah, Poor Bird/Beaux Yeux" (throughout the melody)
Arranged by Betty Bertaux
For two-part treble voices , flute, and oboe (or B-flat clarinet)
Boosey & Hawkes
OCTB6770

61

LESSON 7
TEACHING THE WHOLE NOTE

REMEMBER THAT THE ONE of the most effective ways to teach is to meet the students where they are with the information they already know. So far, your singers know the quarter note, two eighth notes, quarter rest, and half note. They also know how to tie notes together in order to make them sound longer. Draw on this information when you teach the whole note.

Consider using Randall Thompson's beautiful two-part composition "Velvet Shoes," a setting of Elinor Wylie's poem by the same title.

Velvet Shoes

PROCEDURE

Since you are using "Velvet Shoes" to teach a new concept, your singers should already know how to sing the melody well before you begin this strategy, especially if they are very young.

Prepare the board with the following before rehearsal:

A. "Listen and pat a beat on your laps as I sing four measures of 'Velvet Shoes' by myself. In this composition, you will hear one sound on one beat, two sounds on one beat, one sound that lasts for two beats, and a sound that is new. When you hear the new sound, tell me how many sounds it is and how many beats it lasts." (One sound that lasts for four beats.)

B. "Since we already know the half note, or one sound that lasts for two beats, how many half notes will we have to add to the last measure?" Draw two half notes. "What must we do to these half notes to change them into one sound that lasts for four beats?" (Tie them together.)

C. Add the new notation to the rhythm notation on the board.

D. "We have another way to write our new rhythm that is much easier. To make the new rhythm we erase the stems, the tie, and the second note head. This is called 'whole note.' It is one sound that lasts for four beats."

E. "Listen and watch as I clap and sing the rhythm names" (or whatever rhythm tool you have chosen to use). When you demonstrate the clapping for whole note, clap once and hold your hands together for four beats.

64

F. "Everyone clap and sing the rhythm." **Note:** It is important that you guide the singers' reading by clapping as well or by pointing to the rhythm notation. Often, young singers will perform the rhythm by memory without reading the notation. Make sure you reinforce the actual act of musical reading.

G. "Only the sopranos sing the rhythm names as the altos clap and inner hear."

H. "Switch."

I. "Who would like to come up to the board and lead the class by pointing at the rhythms?" Do this several times with different singers.

J. "Turn to the first page of your score. Where do you find the rhythm we have been practicing?" (Measure 17.)

K. "Point to the rhythm in your scores as you sing the rhythm names."

L. "Now sing the words and point to the rhythm."

M. Continue with your rehearsal. As you proceed with rehearsal, make sure you ask your singers to find and identify any additional whole notes to reinforce this new concept.

REINFORCEMENT THROUGH GUIDED SIGHT-READING

Before sight-reading the whole note in the next rehearsal, you should review the whole note and the other known rhythms in the ear portion of your warm-up. For instance, you could play the game "Which rhythm am I clapping?"

Create rhythms similar to the phrase you want your singers to sight-read. For example, the following rhythms set up the first sung rhythm of "Al Shlosha D'varim." Clap them in random order and ask your singers to identify and then perform them. If this is new or difficult for your ensemble, then you should say and clap the rhythms to help them identify the correct ones.

Al Shlosha D'varim

Text by
Pirkei Avot (Mishnah)

Music by
Allan E. Kaplan

PROCEDURE

Immediately following the rhythm reinforcement activity above:

A. "Let's erase all the rhythms except for C. Count and clap this one without my help."

B. "If I make a small change, can you clap the new rhythm?" Change the third beat of the third measure to a quarter note. Ask your singers to clap and count.

C. "Now turn to your score, 'Al Shlosha D'varim,' and tell me in which measure this rhythm begins?" (Measure 5.)
D. "Say and clap the rhythm from your own scores."
E. "Sopranos, clap, and count the rhythm as the altos inner hear. Follow the notes by pointing to them in your scores." It may be helpful to keep the beat on a drum to keep your singers together as well to make sure they do not skip any beats.
F. "Switch."
G. "Everyone point to your scores and say the rhythm names."
H. "Altos, say the rhythm names as the sopranos speak the words of the song." Depending on your singers' reading and language skills, it might help them if you pronounce the words first.

I. "Switch."
J. "Everyone speak the words in rhythm."
K. "Echo me as I sing the words to the melody." Repeat as necessary.

Note: The singular focus of this strategy is to sight-read rhythms and not sight-read the melody. In this exercise, the singers learn the melody by rote. If your singers are advanced and have the melodic skills, and you have time in your rehearsal, you should certainly sight-read the melody. One way to accomplish this is by adding the solfa letters below the rhythm notation.

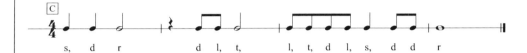

L. Continue with the rest of your rehearsal.

Reminder: The end of each strategy always has a practice, or repetition, element. This is a crucial step. Naming the new concept is only one part of the teaching process. In the practice portion, you make sure the singers repeatedly hear and perform each new concept. Watch and listen carefully and critically. Praise your singers and ask them questions that will lead them to correct any mistakes. By repeating the practice activities, you make sure that they will remember them for the next rehearsal.

SUGGESTED COMPOSITIONS

"Morning Star" (measures 12–17)
Words and music by Vera Kistler
Two-part vocal with piano
Alliance Publications
AP-1034

"God, Who Touches Earth with Beauty" (measures 17–20)
Raymond H. Haan
Soprano and alto voices and piano (with optional handbells, finger cymbals/triangle)
MorningStar Music
MSM-50-9452

LESSON 8
TEACHING LA

TO LEARN L, your singers will hear the new tone, or sound, right above s. Choose a piece of music that the singers know well and ask leading questions about l. For example, I will use "Li'l Liza Jane" (see the chapter "Building a Foundation") to demonstrate how to teach l and use the lighthearted composition "Things I Learned from a Cow" as a tool for reinforcement and sight-reading.

PROCEDURE

Write the following on the board before rehearsal begins:

And

s
m
r
d

Add f if your singers know it.

A. End the warm-up portion of your rehearsal by singing a vocalise or echo-singing activity that includes the known tone set drm s, in the key of D major.

B. Tell your singers: "Listen carefully as I sing a song you know on [lu], that has a new sound in it. Raise your hands when you hear this new tone that is different from drm and s. This song begins on m." **Note:** I always sing, not speak, the solfa names in order to reinforce their corresponding sounds.

C. "Listen as I sing it again, and tell me if it is a higher or lower sound." (Higher.)

D. "Yes, the new tone is higher than s. Listen again, and tell me if this sound is close to or far apart from s. That is, is it a step or skip higher?" (Close; step higher.)

E. Draw the singers' attention to the staff on the board and say, "Look at the board. If s is here on the second space, and the new sound is a step higher, where will we place it on the staff?" (On the third line.)

F. "I'll draw in the new note on the staff, and then sing the song again with the new name and hand sign. Watch and listen carefully."

G. "Now everyone sing with the new name and hand sign."

H. "Only the sopranos sing with solfa and hand signs, and altos inner hear and show all the hand signs."

I. "Now the altos sing with solfa and hand signs as the sopranos inner hear and show hand signs."

J. "Everyone sing with solfa and hand signs."

K. "Let's now add l to the tone ladder." (Write l.) "Echo me after I sing the tone set up and down, with solfa and hand signs." (Singers perform the entire tone set.)

L. "Can you sing the verse of 'Li'l Liza Jane' by memory with solfa and hand signs?" (All sing.)

M. "Sing the whole song with the words."

Now that the choristers know drm sl, you can now introduce the concept of d pentatonic. Simply define it as a scale or tone set of a melody that has these five notes and ends on d.

Reminder: It's always good to end an exercise using the words since it returns the music to its original intent—a song! These folk songs and choral compositions are pieces of art that were never intended to become technical, theoretical exercises. By singing them with the words at the end of the activity, we are returning them to art.

REINFORCEMENT THROUGH GUIDED SIGHT-SINGING

Things I Learned From A Cow

words and "moosic" by
Valerie Showers Crescenz,
ASCAP

PROCEDURE

Prepare the board with the following before the singers arrive for rehearsal:

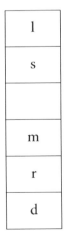

And

d m s s s s   l m d___   r   r   m r m r___

(If your singers are advanced, you should omit writing the solfa letters under the staff.)

A. End the ear-training portion of your warm-up with a practice activity that reinforces the known tone set in the key of D major. The activity should include singing solfa and showing hand signs from the tone ladder and staff notation on the board. Make sure you reinforce patterns similar to the melodic motifs in "Things I Learned from a Cow." These may include:
drmslsmrd
drmdms
slsmrd
slsmd
slmd
drmrmr

B. "Inner hear the solfa and show hand signs as I point to the new song on the board" (the second phrase from "Things I Learned from a Cow"). As the singers perform this task, assess how accurately they are able to do it. Work on any difficulties they may have by asking questions about the names of the solfa. Remember to point to the melody in the composed rhythm.

C. "Let's try it again." The singers perform as above. "Raise your hand if you were able to hear the melody while inner hearing." This is a good way to encourage them to develop their inner hearing, a very important skill. Tell your singers not to be discouraged if they are not hearing it yet. The more they practice this skill, the easier the hearing will become.

D. "Everyone sing aloud with solfa and hand signs as I point to the staff again."

E. "Only the sopranos sing this time."

F. "Only the altos sing."

G. "Is there a soloist who can sing it as I point?" (Solo student sings with solfa and hand signs. Give a lot of praise!)

H. "Who else would like to try by yourself or by choosing a partner to sing with you?"

I. "Everyone sing with solfa and hand signs."

J. "Turn to 'Things I Learned from a Cow.' Who can tell me where this phrase is in the score?" (Just before measure 10.)

K. "Sing the solfa from your score."

L. "Sing the words from the score."

M. Continue with your rehearsal.

Reminder: Whenever you introduce something new to your singers, try to find the concept in other short excerpts in the same or different compositions to reinforce and apply the new information. The singers can echo-sing the new patterns from you, or even sight-read them, depending on their skill level.

REINFORCEMENT THROUGH READING A SONG FROM THE STAFF FOR THE VERY YOUNG

Very young beginners will enjoy reading song-games they already know in choral arrangements. *Songs of a Summer Afternoon* contains four well-known folk songs: "Here Comes a Bluebird"; "Bow Wow Wow"; " I've Been to Harlem"; and "Sailing on the Ocean." Choose one of the first two folk songs—both work well—as an option to reinforce l.

PROCEDURE

Prepare the board with the following before the singers arrive for rehearsal. With younger singers, consider writing d on the staff instead of the treble clef to show them where d is on the staff.

A. Begin by saying to the singers, "Let's all sing 'Here Comes a Bluebird' with the words of the song."

B. State the objective by saying, "Today we will learn to sing this song with the solfa [or 'melody names'] and hand signs."

C. Review the staff placement of all the solfa names.
   1. Point to the staff on the board and ask the singers, "Where is d on the staff today?" (First space.) "Who can volunteer to come to the board to point to all the notes that we will sing as d?"
   2. Review r by saying, "If r is a step higher than d, where is it on the staff?" (Second line.) "Someone come to the board and point to all the notes we will sing as r."
   3. Continue in this way, defining how much higher each note is than the previous, until all the notes are named and identified on the staff.

D. Point to the first note head and ask, "What solfa does our song begin on?" (s).

E. "Show the hand signs and sing the solfa with your inner voice (that is, inner hear) as I point." Point to only as many notes in the rhythm of the song as you know your singers will be able to do well. For example, you might point to only the first five or ten notes if they are very inexperienced.

F. "Now sing it aloud with solfa and hand signs as I point." Continue until they are able to sing the entire melody.

G. Practice the reading from the staff by asking a student leader to come to the board to lead the ensemble. Repeat this many times.

H. Remember to ask smaller groups, trios, duets, and soloists to sing to practice this new skill.

I. "Now sing the words."

In the next rehearsal you might practice the same song again to reinforce l by writing the same melody on the board with the solfa letter below each note.

s   s   l   s   m   s   s   l   s   m   m   r   r   r   r   d   m   d

Review the song by singing the solfa from the board. Next, ask the singers to copy the solfa letters underneath the notes in their own scores. They can then sing the solfa from their own notation as they point to each note on the staff.

Visit the companion website to download additional sight-reading exercises.

SUGGESTED COMPOSITIONS

"Peace Like a River" (soprano part, measures 81–94)
Composed and arranged by Douglas Beam
Two-part voices with piano accompaniment
Colla Voce Music
24-96400

"Cherry Riddle Song" (soprano part, measures 10–13)
Arranged by Judy Herrington
Two-part voices with piano accompaniment
Pavane Publishing
P1016

THE FOLLOWING LESSON to teach f by itself assumes that your singers already know drm sl. End the ear-training portion of your warm-up with an echo-singing activity reinforcing the known tone set. Then move on to the following procedure, which leads your singers to discover the new tone f.

Select a composition similar to the many arrangements of the American folk song "Coffee Grows on White Oak Trees." The one referred to below is a two-part treble setting by Vernon Sanders.

Coffee Grows on White Oak Trees

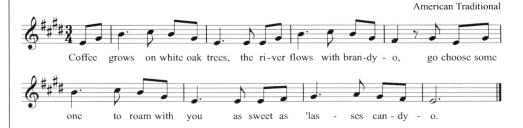

American Traditional

Coffee grows on white oak trees, the ri-ver flows with bran-dy - o, go choose some one to roam with you as sweet as 'las - ses can-dy - o.

Notice, in the last system of the melody in the second to last measure, that there is an f (the pitch A) in a mfm context. This is where the singers will discover the new tone.

PROCEDURE

Prepare the board with the following before the singers arrive for rehearsal:

Lead your singers through an echo-singing activity during the ear development of the warm-up that reinforces drm sl and known melodic patterns from "Coffee Grows on White Oak Trees." Make sure you perform it in the key of E major. Refer to the appendix for suggestions. The singers should already know how to sing the melody of the composition before you begin the procedure.

A. Say to your singers: "Listen carefully as I sing the melody of 'Coffee Grows on White Oak Trees' on [lu]. Raise your hands when you hear a sound that is different from drm s and l." Remember to sing the names of the solfa with their corresponding sounds as you give this instruction. This way you continually reinforce the names of the solfa with their corresponding sounds. (Singers will raise hands on the new tone.)

B. "Let's isolate the phrase where this new sound happens. If this phrase begins on d, what can you tell me about the new sound? Which note is it closest to? Is it higher or lower than that note?" Sing the entire phrase above on [lu]. (Singers should respond that it is close to m and higher.)

C. "If m is on the second line, where will we write the new sound on the staff if it is just above m?" (Second space.) Write the new sound on the staff.

D. "Listen again as I sing this phrase with the new sound's name and hand sign."

E. "Everyone sing the phrase with solfa and the hand sign." Practice this with smaller groups and soloists, ending with everyone.

F. "Turn to the first page of music in 'Coffee Grows on White Oak Trees.' Tell me where you find this phrase in your score." (Just before letter A.)

G. "Sing this phrase with solfa from your own score."

H. "Sing the words."

I. Proceed with the rest of the rehearsal.

REINFORCEMENT THROUGH GUIDED SIGHT-READING

Building on what the singers now know, you can immediately apply their new skill in the same rehearsal by briefly mentioning and singing it in another pattern in the same song, or by applying it to another composition, as was done earlier with "Glory to God" in lesson 5B. In a future rehearsal the choristers can reinforce f in a longer, more focused activity.

For example, sight-read f in a composition similar to the Italian carol "Dormi, Dormi." This procedure assumes the singers already know drmfsl.

PROCEDURE

A. As a warm-up exercise, ask your singers to perform the composition from which they learned f. Make sure they perform it in F major, regardless of the original key signature. Singing it in F major will tune the singers in the same key as "Dormi, Dormi."

B. From staff notation on the board, ask the choristers to sing various patterns with solfa and hand signs as you point to the notes on the staff. To set them up for success, point to patterns that are similar to the ones the singers will encounter in "Dormi, Dormi."

C. Say to the singers, as you draw their attention to the staff with the entire melody written on it, "Now, inner hear [audiate] this new melody as I point to the notes on the staff." If you know your singers will have difficulty with the entire excerpt, perform this step in shorter phrases.

Dormi, Dormi, melody only

D. Check to see if they are actually hearing the melody by saying, "Raise your hands if you are able to hear the melody with your inner hearing."

E. Repeat the inner hear activity as you hum a few notes in the excerpt to help the singers' inner hearing. At the same time you are pointing, make sure you are also watching the singers to ensure that they are showing the correct hand signs.

F. Repeat the inner hearing activity as necessary. As you point, hum or sing with solfa different notes from the ones you sang before.

G. "Now everyone sing aloud with solfa and hand signs."

H. Practice the reading skill by asking half the ensemble to sing aloud as the other half shows hand signs and inner hears. Repeat the practice many times, working your way down to smaller groups, duets, and even solos. End by asking everyone to sing the solfa.

I. "Now turn to the first page of 'Dormi, Dormi.' Sing the solfa as you point to the notes in your own scores." Repeat as necessary.

J. "Let's look at the words. Most of the time, how many notes do you see for each syllable?" (One.) "What measures have a syllable of a word that has two notes?" (Measures 12 and 14.). "What syllable has two notes?" (Di.)

K. Ask half of the group to sing solfa and the other to sing the words.

L. Switch.

M. End by asking all the singers to sing the words.

SUGGESTED COMPOSITIONS

"My Shadow" (first eight measures of the melody)
Dominic DiOrio
Text by Robert Louis Stevenson
Unison voices with piano
Roger Dean Publishing
15/2330R

"Japanese Snow Song" (measures 4–12)
Arranged by Lois Brownsley and Marti Lantz
Two-part with piano
Alfred Music Publishing
27320

LESSON 10
TEACHING FOUR SIXTEENTH NOTES

YOUR SINGERS NOW KNOW that there can be one, and two, and no sounds on one beat. Hearing four sounds on one beat will lead them to discover four sixteenth notes.

Find a melody in your repertoire of folk songs, vocalises, or choral compositions that your singers know well. For example, consider using the first few phrases of "S'vivon." Betty Bertaux has written a wonderful choral arrangement of this traditional melody.

S'VIVON

Traditional Hebrew Song

PROCEDURE

Prepare the board with the following before the singers arrive for rehearsal. Remember, when you prepare the board, always omit the new concept.

A. Begin your rehearsal by reviewing and singing a phrase of a familiar piece of music ("Mrs. Jenny Wren," for example) while clapping and counting the known rhythms. As another option, you can perform an echo clapping activity. Refer to the appendix for more ideas.

B. "We can hear and perform one and two sounds on a beat: quarter note and two eighth notes [or ta and ti-ti, depending on the system of rhythm names that you use with your ensemble]. Pat the beat on your laps and listen carefully as I sing a song that you know. There is a new rhythm in this song. Let's see what we can discover about it." Singers pat the beat as you sing the words of "S'vivon" for the first eight measures only.

C. Then, repeat with beat and rhythm together. Say, "Sopranos, pat the beat as the altos sing and clap the rhythm of the song. Sing only as far as I did. Remember to listen for a rhythm that is different from one or two sounds on a beat."

D. Switch groups.

E. "I'll keep the beat on a drum as you all sing the words. Raise your hands when you think you hear the new rhythm."

F. "When the new rhythm occurs, how many sounds do you hear on one beat?" (Four.) In the example on the board, draw in four vertical lines where the rhythm occurs. "Since they occur on one beat, we add a beam across the top of the four sounds." Draw a single beam. "And since they are fast sounds, we add another beam." Draw the second beam.

G. "Listen as I clap and sing the rhythm name [or counting] for our new rhythm, called four sixteenth notes."

H. "Everyone clap and sing the rhythm as I point to the notes on the board."

I. "Altos, sing the rhythm with the rhythm names as the sopranos clap the rhythm and inner hear the names."

J. Switch groups.

K. Repeat with smaller groups, soloists, and student leaders. Ask them to go to the board and point to the rhythm notation. End with everyone performing together.

L. "Take out 'S'vivon' and look at the first page of music. Can you still sing the rhythm names as you point to the notes on the page?"

M. "Sing the words as you point to the rhythms in your own score."

N. Continue with the rest of the rehearsal. Throughout the rest of rehearsal, make sure you find and identify four sixteenth notes in other compositions to reinforce this new concept.

You can now practice four sixteenth notes along with the rest of the rhythms your singers know. Once you teach a new rhythm, it never goes away. Rather, it is added to your singers' body of knowledge and must be continually practiced in a variety of creative ways, including sight-reading. Refer to the appendix for suggested activities.

REINFORCEMENT THROUGH GUIDED SIGHT-READING

Select from your repertoire a composition that has the new rhythm prevalent in a short phrase or phrases; for example, "Aussie Rhythms."

The sight-reading will focus on the second voice part beginning in measure 31. You will notice there is a rhythm combination of eighth note and eighth rest. If you haven't done so already, this is a good time to introduce the eighth rest.

Aussie Animals

Original Words and Music &
Arrangement by David Lawrence

laugh,   kook - a - bur - ra,   gay   your   life   must   be!

laugh,   kook - a - bur - ra,   gay   your   life   must   be!

PROCEDURE

Write the rhythm of the excerpt from the second voice part on the board before the singers arrive for rehearsal.

A. Ask the singers to review a known composition in which the four sixteenth note pattern exists. This composition can be the one from which they originally discovered the rhythm. They should sing it first on the words, then end with clapping and counting.

B. Point to the excerpt from "Aussie Animals" on the board and ask them the number of times the sixteenth note pattern occurs. (Eight times.)

C. Ask the singers to clap and count the rhythm according to their skill level. If they are beginners perform only two measures at a time. They can read the entire excerpt if they are more experienced.

D. Practice the reading by asking smaller groups, trios, duets, and soloists to perform as you or another singer points to the rhythms on the board.

E. Ask the singers to read the words in rhythm according to their ability level. This will include reading the words that you write under the excerpt or reading the words from their scores.

1. Half the group counts the rhythm as the other half speaks the words. Repeat as necessary as you switch which group performs the rhythm or the words.

2. All speak the words as they clap the rhythm.

F. Teach the melody by rote. If the singers know the solfa for the tone set, dmfsl, ask them to echo it back after you sing.

G. Tell the singers to turn to measure 31 in "Aussie Animals." Ask them to sing and clap the rhythm as they count and point to their own scores. Repeat as necessary.

H. End the activity by asking the choristers to perform the words.

 Visit the companion website to download additional sight-reading exercises.

LESSON 11
INTRODUCING HIGH DO

I RECOMMEND USING the folk song "Li'l Liza Jane" to introduce d' to your singers. Write the song on the board in staff notation, omitting d'. You will add it to the staff later as you lead your singers to discover this new tone. If your singers are young you may consider writing in the solfege below the notation. Erase it as they become fluent with the names.

PROCEDURE

A. Ask all your singers to perform only the verse with solfa, without any help from you.

B. Tell your singers: "Sing the verse again, but this time stop and sustain (or hold) the last note of the verse. I will go on to the first note of the refrain." (Perform.) "As you compare the note you sustained to the note I sang, what can you tell me about what you heard?" (The two tones sound the same, and the one you are singing is higher.)

C. Name the new tone "high d" and add the note to the staff. Draw a tone ladder on the board and say to your students as you add "d'" above l that the apostrophe at the top right side of the letter is to indicate that this is a higher d than the one they already know: it is "high d."

D. Sing the entire song with solfa and hand signs.

E. Point to l on the staff and say, "Where is l on the staff?" (Third line.) "Now look at high d. "Where did we write it on the staff?" (Fourth line.). Ask, "Is high d a step or a skip higher than l?" (Skip.)

F. Ask all the singers to perform the entire song with solfa and hand signs. Practice with smaller groups and soloists. End with everyone.

G. Finally, end with everyone singing the words of the song.

REINFORCEMENT THROUGH GUIDED SIGHT-READING

Extract phrases that contain the singers' known melodic tone set from your ensemble's repertoire for sight-reading. In the following exercise, I assume the singers know drm sl d', and I demonstrate the procedure for sight-reading using Benjamin Britten's beautiful arrangement of "The Sally Gardens." The procedure will also demonstrate how to morph, or gradually change a known song, "Liza Jane," into the melody found in "The Sally Gardens."

Analyzing the first eight measures of the voice part of "The Sally Gardens," you will find that there are two identical phrases, each four measures long. Looking closer, you will also find two motifs that make up each phrase. Each motif lasts for two measures.

And

Sight-reading the motifs separately will be much easier for your beginning singers. Keep this in mind as you plan lessons for future, similar procedures.

Prepare the board with the following before the singers arrive for rehearsal:

d'
l
s
m
r
d

Include the final phrase of "Li'l Liza Jane" in staff notation (see step D in the following procedure).

PROCEDURE

A. Ask everyone to sing "Li'l Liza Jane" with solfa and hand signs in the key of D-flat major.

B. Everyone now sings the scale with solfa as you point to the
   1. Tone ladder
   2. Staff notation

C. First motif:
   1. Ask everyone to sing the solfa as you point to the tone ladder in the rhythm of the motif.
   2. Everyone sings the solfa as you point to the scale staff notation in the rhythm of the motif.
   3. Finally, everyone sings solfa as you point to the original notation of the motif.

D. Second motif:
   1. Using the last phrase from the refrain of "Li'l Liza Jane," gradually change the rhythm and melody by erasing and adding to the staff notation until it becomes "The Sally Gardens." Ask everyone to sing the solfa after each change as you point to the staff. If your ensemble is advanced, they should sing the solfa without the solfa letters written underneath the staff.

E. Ask everyone to sing both motifs together with solfa as you point to the staffs on the board.

F. Ask everyone to sing from their own scores with
1. Solfa
2. Text

REINFORCEMENT THROUGH ADDITIONAL SIGHT-READING ACTIVITY FOCUSING ON INNER HEARING

Assuming that your singers know l, drm sl d', another option for practice of d' is found in the arrangement of folk songs in *Sail Away*. Analysis of soprano I in measures 13–22 shows that d' is approached and left by its pentatonic neighbor, l, the easiest context for sight-reading.

Sail Away

Arranged by
Susan Brumfield

PROCEDURE

Prepare the board with the following before the singers arrive for rehearsal:

A. Tune-up activity: Improvise four-beat simple melodic patterns in F major that begin to approximate some of the melodic motifs found in *Sail Away*.

   1. Point to the scale staff notation and sing solfa as the singers echo with solfa and hand signs.

   2. Point to the scale staff notation and sing [lu] as the singers echo you with solfa and hand signs.

   3. Point to the scale staff notation without singing and ask the choristers to inner hear. They then sing back with solfa and hand signs.

B. Sight-reading *Sail Away*: Sight-read the melody from the staff notation on the board according to the choristers' ability level.

   1. If the singers are beginners, point to only two measures at a time, in rhythm, and ask the singers to inner hear (audiate) and show the hand signs. They then immediately sing the pattern back. Finally, put all the measures together.

2. If the singers are more advanced, point in longer phrases as they audiate and show hand signs. You can do this in two two-measure phrases at a time, or the entire eight-measure excerpt. They should sing the phrase(s) back immediately after audiating.

C. Ask the choristers to turn to *Sail Away*, pages 1 and 2, and to say in which measure and voice part they find the excerpt they learned on the board. (Soprano I, beginning in measure 13.)

D. Ask the singers to point to the melody in their own scores and sing the solfa. Repeat this as necessary as you help individuals read their own scores.

E. Finally, ask the singers to sing the words.

SUGGESTED COMPOSITION

"Little David, Play on Your Harp" (soprano part, measures 3–7)
Spiritual
Arranged by Emily Crocker
Jenson Publications
47123013

LESSON 12
TEACHING THE EIGHTH NOTE
WITH TWO SIXTEENTH NOTES

IN THIS PROCEDURE, the singers should already know how to sing the melody of "Old Joe Clark," or a similar melody in which the eighth note with two sixteenth notes are prevalent throughout. The singers will discover a "new" rhythm consisting of three sounds on one beat. They will be able to hear and describe that the first sound is slow, or long, and the last two sounds are faster, or shorter.

Old Joe Clark

PROCEDURE

Prepare the singers with an echo-clapping activity that reviews their known rhythms.

A. Ear:

1. Ask your singers to perform the first eight measures of "Old Joe Clark" from memory, using the words of the song.

2. Ask half of the chorus to pat the beat and listen to the rhythm while the other half claps the rhythm and sings the words.

3. Switch the groups' roles.

4. Tell your singers: "Everyone listen and pat the beat as I sing the words and clap the rhythm by myself. Sometimes you will hear one and two sounds on a beat, and other times you will even hear one sound that lasts for two beats. Listen carefully for something different on one beat. When it is different, how many sounds do you hear on that single beat?" Perform as directed and repeat as necessary. Singers should respond that they hear three sounds on one beat.

5. "Raise your hands when you hear me sing the beat that contains three sounds." Perform and assess whether they are hearing the new rhythm in the correct places.

6. "What words do you hear when there are three sounds on a beat?" ("Plung, plunka.")

7. "Listen again and tell me if the sounds are three even sounds or if some of them might be faster." Sing again. Your singers should say the sounds are not even, and there are faster sounds.

8. "Listen again and tell me where the faster sounds occur. Are they at the beginning of the beat or at the end?" (End.)

B. Visual representation:

1. "On the board, I drew most of the rhythms for 'Old Joe Clark.' The beats where you see nothing drawn contain our new rhythm."

2. "Let's now draw our new rhythm in the beats where they occur." Draw in the three sounds in the correct places, spacing the last two sounds close to each other.

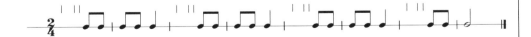

3. "Now, since these three sounds occur on the same beat, we can beam them all together." Draw a single beam across the top of all three stems.

91

4. "And since the last two sounds are faster, we will add a second beam." Draw a second beam across the last two sounds. **Note:** Draw on the singers' own knowledge if you have already taught them four sixteenth notes. Ask them if they remember what was added to show that they were fast sounds. The singers should respond that a second beam was added to the rhythm.

C. Name the new rhythm and practice:

1. "We call these three uneven sounds on one beat 'ti-tiri' [or whatever name from the system you choose to use]. Listen as I clap and sing the names for the rhythm."
2. "Everyone clap and sing the names for the rhythms."
3. Practice with smaller groups and solos, and end with everyone together.

D. Application to the score:
1. "Take out 'Old Joe Clark.' Can you still sing the rhythm names from your own score as you point to the rhythm on the staff?"
2. "Now sing the words."

REINFORCEMENT THROUGH GUIDED SIGHT-READING

A good way to practice this new rhythm is to develop lessons in which your singers sight-read the rhythm within your current repertoire. For example, you may use Franz Joseph Haydn's "Gloria" from his *Heiligmesse*, or a similar composition.

Gloria

PROCEDURE

A. Preparatory warm-up: create large cards with the following five rhythms written on them and place tape on the back of each one. Place the cards in mixed order on the shelf of your board. Clap the rhythms and ask your singers to identify the one you clap. Then place the cards in order on the board. Clap them in this order: A, E, C, B, D. Once the rhythm is identified and put in place, your singers should clap and count (or say the rhythm names) for each individual rhythm.

B. Ask your singers: "As I point to them, can you clap and count all five in the new order without stopping?"

C. Remove cards A, B, and C from the board, leaving only the following:

D. "Clap and count the rhythms I have left on the board."

E. Ask smaller groups and soloists to count and clap as you point to the notation. Choose individuals to go to the board to point and lead the ensemble as all clap and count.

F. "Turn to 'Gloria' and look at the rhythm of your part on the first page. What do you notice about the rhythm you see in your score?" (It is the same as the rhythm we practiced on the board.)

G. "Count the rhythm as you point to your notes in your own score."

H. "Sopranos, continue to count the rhythm as the altos speak the words underneath each note."

I. "Switch."

J. "Everyone point to the rhythm on the staff as you speak the words under the staff."

K. Continue with the rest of your rehearsal.

INTRODUCING AND SIGHT-READING TWO SIXTEENTH NOTES WITH AN EIGHTH NOTE

Once the choristers know the pattern of the eighth note with two sixteenth notes, it is simple to introduce two sixteenths with an eighth note. They will easily hear that there are three uneven sounds on one beat, with the two fast sounds at the beginning of the beat.

Sight-reading the two combinations of these rhythms should be easy. A composition similar to "Ezekiel and David" is a good choice to reinforce them.

Ezekiel and David

Traditional Spirituals
Arranged by Sally K. Albrecht

PROCEDURE

Prepare the board with the following before the singers arrive for rehearsal:

A. Begin with an echo-clapping activity that practices the rhythms found in the excerpt. For example:

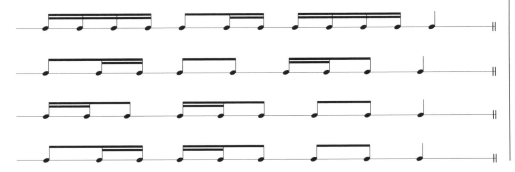

1. Ask the singers to clap and count the rhythms in order from the board after you, as you
   a. Clap and count
   b. Clap but do not count
2. Clap the rhythms in random order and ask the singers to identify which rhythm you clapped. They then clap and count it back to you.

B. Point to the excerpt from "Ezekiel" on the board and ask them, "What do you notice about the rhythm patterns in the first three measures?" (They are the same.)

C. Ask the singers to sight-read the rhythm according to their skill level. If they are beginners ask them to clap and count one measure at a time. If they are more advanced ask them to clap and count all four measures.

D. Practice the reading by asking half the ensemble to count as the other side claps, and switch. Ask smaller groups, trios, duets, and soloists to perform. Ask singers who are doing well to go to the board to lead the ensemble by pointing to each note, and so on.

E. "Turn to pages 4 and 5 of "Ezekiel and David." In which voice part and measure do you find the rhythm from the board?" (Part 1, measure 9.)

F. "Count the rhythm from your own score as you point to the notes on the staff."

G. Ask half of the chorus to count as the other half speaks the words in rhythm. Switch.

H. "Everyone, speak the words to the rhythm from your own scores."

I. You can then teach the melody by rote by asking them to follow the notes as you sing.

Note: If the singers are younger, consider writing the words underneath the rhythm on the board so that you can provide more guidance in adding the text.

 Visit the companion website to download additional sight-reading exercises.

SUGGESTED COMPOSITIONS

"J'entends Le Moulin" ("I Hear the Windmill") (eighth note and two sixteenth notes rhythm is prevalent throughout)
French Canadian folk song
Arranged by Emily Crocker
Hal Leonard Corporation
08551983

Appalachian Dances (two sixteenth notes with eighth notes, measures 67–70)
Appalachian folk songs
Arranged by Cristi Cary Miller
Hal Leonard Corporation
08564224

"Al-yadil yadil yadi"
Palestinian folk song
Arranged by John Higgins
For two-part treble and piano
Hal Leonard Corporation
08745597

LESSON 13
TEACHING LOW LA

SINCE WE EXPANDED the tone set with d' and your singers now know drm(f) sl d', adding the tones below d will be quite simple. Your singers have just learned that there is another higher d. They will now discover other tones that are lower and that they have some of the same names they already know. Keep in mind that they know that d' is a skip higher than l. This knowledge base makes it easy to discover the name of l, on their own with logical guiding questions.

The singers do not have to know d' in order to learn l,. See step E in the following procedure.

The composition "Things I Learned from a Cow," used earlier to teach l, can also be used to teach l,. If you are to effectively use the excerpt to teach the new tone, your singers should already know how to sing the first couple of phrases well and in tune from memory without your help.

Things I Learned From A Cow

words and "moosic" by
Valerie Showers Crescenz,
ASCAP

PROCEDURE

Prepare the board with the following before the singers arrive at rehearsal:

And

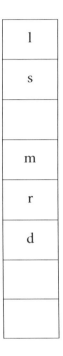

A. Review the known tone set by singing the second phrase of "Things I Learned from a Cow" (or another similar composition) with solfa and hand signs. Your singers can sing it from the board in staff notation or from their own scores.

B. Say to your singers: "Listen carefully as I sing the first phrase by myself on [lu]. Raise your hand when you hear a note that is different from drm sl. This phrase begins on m." **Reminder:** The singers should be able to hear the new tone. If they cannot, you should not proceed. Instead, practice the known tone set until it becomes a more fluent part of their hearing. They need more reinforcement of the known tone set if they cannot hear something different.

C. "Was the new sound higher or lower?" (Lower.)

D. "Listen again and tell me if you think it is a step or skip lower than d." (Skip lower.) This might be difficult for them to hear. If so, provide a visual representation by playing the melody on a resonator bell ladder so they can see the skip.

99

E. "We already know the name of a note that is a skip lower than d. What is it?" (l). "Yes, this is l, too, and since it is lower than d we will call it 'low l.'" Draw l, in the tone ladder to show that it is a skip lower than d. **Note:** They do not have to know d' in order to learn l,. Reformat the beginning of this step without the comparison to d'.

F. "Sing only the first two measures from the board with solfa and hand signs. Can you describe where d is on the staff?" (On the space below the staff.)

G. "So, if d is on a space, and l, is a skip lower, will l, be on a line or a space?" (On a space.)

H. If you have not already done so, this is the time to introduce ledger lines. Define them as lines and spaces that can be added above and below the staff to create higher and lower pitches. "In order to have a space for l, we have to draw a ledger line below the staff." Draw the ledger line.

I. "Now that we have the ledger line below the staff, the space for l, will be just below it." Draw in the note for l,.

J. At this point, since your singers have been through many lessons and procedures, you, as teacher, can now begin to demonstrate less and ask your singers to perform the new concepts right away and on their own. "Now sing from the board with solfa and hand signs as I point to the music notation. When you show the hand sign for l,, remember that it is lower than d."

K. Reinforce the concept in smaller groups of singers and soloists performing with solfa and hand signs. Ask singers to go to the board to point to the notation and lead the ensemble. End with everyone singing the solfa from the board.

L. "Open your scores. Can you still sing the solfa from your own notation?"

M. "Now sing the words."

N. Continue with your rehearsal. Throughout the rest of rehearsal, make sure to reinforce l, again in the same or another composition. Singing the tone in a very short phrase, even only three or four notes, at a later time is a good way to practice. This reinforcement will allow your singers to remember it more fluently.

REINFORCEMENT OF LOW LA, THROUGH AN INNER HEARING ACTIVITY

As you have done for previous new melodic concepts, you should also apply your singers' new knowledge of l, to a guided sight-reading activity. Use short phrases in other compositions in your repertoire. In addition, incorporate some melodic practice activities (see the appendix) into the ear-training portion of your warm-up.

For example, practice inner hearing, or audiation, in a well-known composition. Choose a melody similar to the traditional spiritual "Mary Had a Baby" (in *Born, Born in Bethlehem*, arranged by Donald Moore), review the melody with both the words and solfa, and ask the singers to inner hear some of the notes.

PROCEDURE

Prepare the board with the following before the singers arrive for rehearsal:

Mary Had a Baby

And

l
s
m
r
d
l,

A. Ask the singers to review the melody of "Born, Born in Bethlehem" by
   1. Singing the words without your help. **Note:** If they can do this well then you can proceed with the activity. If not, work more with the singers until they know the melody well.
   2. Review the staff placement for all the melodic tones on the staff excerpt on the board and ask the singers to sing the melody by themselves with solfa and hand signs as you point to the notes.

B. Ask the singers to show all of the hand signs for the entire melody as they inner hear the following tones. Even though they are inner hearing notes, they should still show the hand sign. In this step, they will sing the melody seven times, each repetition inner hearing different solfa:
   1. r
   2. m
   3. m and r
   4. d
   5. d, r, and m
   6. l,
   7. All the tones

C. End the activity by singing aloud all the solfa with hand signs.

D. Sing the words of the melody.

LOOKING AHEAD

Once l, is added, you can easily add s, and other lower tones, as well as introducing the concept of l, pentatonic. Now the singers can perform "Canoe Song" with solfa. Once you add f and t to the tone set, your singers will know ltdrmfsl, or the natural minor scale. Refer to the teaching of natural minor in lesson 18. Using l as a tonic for natural minor is a simple tool because the whole and half steps are in the correct place without the use of any chromatic solfa names. When d is used as the tonic, altered solfege is required to accommodate the order of the whole and half steps within the scale: drmefsleted. Having said this, make sure that you use the tool that makes the most sense to you and your singers. There are many ways to teach our singers, as long as our use of the tools is consistent.

SUGGESTED COMPOSITION

"Ain'-a That Good News?" (measures 9–12)
African-American spiritual
Arranged by Mark Patterson
Unison/two-part with piano
Choristers Guild
CGA1029

LESSON 14
TEACHING TI

THIS LESSON FOR TEACHING t can come earlier in the melodic sequence, depending on your ensemble's repertoire. For instance, it can be taught after drmfs or even drm, since t, is a neighbor tone to d. Remember, all of these lessons can be rearranged, as long as the discovery of the new information flows in a logical way.

The easiest melodic context to teach t is when it occurs as a lower neighbor to d: dt,d. A good example of this context is found in the melody of the Czech canon "Friendship Song" (edited and arranged for four voices with an added descant by Doreen Rao). It is the same melody as "Come Let's Dance," a traditional song found in the beginning of this book in the introductory chapter "Building a Foundation." "White Sand and Gray Sand," the English street cry in "Building a Foundation," also works well. Whatever composition you choose to use for introducing t, make sure the song is already in your singers' ears and they know it well before beginning the procedure.

Friendship Song

♩ = 120 (feeling in 1, not 3)
1,2,3,& 4 in unison

Czech Canon
Edited & Arranged by Doreen Rao

Sing of friend-ship, shin-ing gold-en treas-ure. Friend-ship is the key to love and joy.

PROCEDURE

Write the following on the board before rehearsal. Notice that t, (D-sharp) is omitted from the staff notation since it is the new tone your singers will discover. Include all the notes your singers know in the tone ladder. This example assumes they already know drmfs. Because they already know f, they should already know the concept of half step, since they learned it in the f procedure.

And

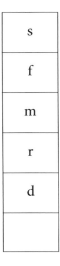

And

A. Begin the ear-training portion of your warm-up with a practice activity using the singers' known tone set. For example, you may choose echo-singing.

    1. Sing solfa and show hand signs for various patterns, and ask your singers to sing back with solfa and hand signs. For example:

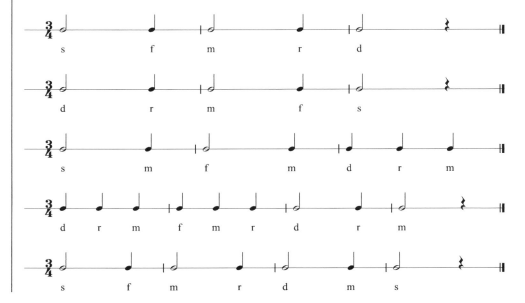

2. Sing the above patterns (or other similar patterns) on [lu] while showing hand signs as your singers sing back with solfa and hand signs.

3. Sing the patterns on [lu] without hand signs as your singers sing back with solfa and hand signs.

B. "Listen carefully as I sing a song you know. Raise your hand when you hear a new sound, or a note that is different from drmf and s." Your singers should raise their hands twice at the appropriate times. If they are unable to hear the new sound, then you should slow down and work more on drmfs until that tone set is a more fluent part of the singers' hearing. If they are able to hear the new sound, you can proceed.

C. "Is the new sound higher or lower than drmfs?" (Lower.)

D. "Listen again, and see if you can tell me if it is a step or skip lower than d. In other words, does it sound close to d or far away?" (Close to d, a step lower.)

E. "Look at the melody of 'Friendship Song' on the board. If d (point to d in the third measure) is on the first line, where on the staff should we write the new sound that is a step lower?" (The space underneath the staff.) Write the note in both places on the staff.

F. "Listen and watch carefully as I sing the entire melody with the new note name and hand sign." You should sing the melody with the solfa and show the hand signs below each note on the board to guide the singers' reading. This is crucial for beginners, since they will often perform from memory instead of reading. You have to make sure they are associating the sounds with the visual symbols by actually reading the musical notation.

G. "Everyone sing the solfa and show the new hand sign."

H. "Now we can add t, to the tone ladder." The tone ladder provides an excellent visual representation of the relationship between t, and the rest of the notes.

I. "Let's also look at the piano keyboard. If E equals d, and t, is D-sharp (point to E and D-sharp), what kind of step do we have between d and t,?" (Half step.)

J. Reinforce the new note by having the singers read the staff notation from the board in smaller groups, duets, and soloists. Have them sing the solfa and show the hand signs. In addition, ask students to go to the board and point to the notes to lead the ensemble's performance.

K. "Turn to your 'Friendship Song' scores. Can you still sing the solfa from your own score as you point to each note?"

L. "Now sing your own part with solfa and point to the notes in your score. Begin in measure 9 and stop on the first note of measure 19."
Note: At this place in the score the choral arrangement has the vocal parts performing the melody in canon.

M. "Sing the same music with the words."

N. Continue with the rest of the rehearsal making sure you take brief opportunities to reinforce t by identifying and performing it in different compositions.

Another example of a composition that has t, in a dt,d context is "Kyrie Eleison" by Ron Kean. Follow the same procedures outlined above and excerpt the first two phrases, beginning when the voice part enters in measure 5. Note that both phrases contain dt,d. In order to use "Kyrie Eleison," or another song with the same tone set, the singers will already have to know s, since it occurs in the excerpted phrases.

Kyrie Eleison

Ron Kean

REINFORCEMENT THROUGH SIGHT-READING IN TWO PARTS FROM STAFF NOTATION

In following rehearsals, you should practice t through additional melodic reinforcement activities and through other melodic teaching strategies that will develop your ensemble's reading skills.

For example:

Ich jauchze, ich Lache mit Schall

J.S. Bach
Edited by Doreen Rao

Singing in parallel thirds is difficult for many beginning choruses. Solfa is an effective tool to anchor the singers' ears and make the singing easier.

A. Staff notation tune-up from the board:

1. Tune up the tone set by asking all of your singers to perform solfa with hand signs in unison as you improvise simple melodies in quarter note rhythms and point to the staff notation.

2. Ask them to sing in a two-part canon. The sopranos sing as you point to improvised melodies, and the altos sing the same melodies two notes later. When you improvise melodies using scale, or step motion, the singers will sing in parallel thirds.

3. Inner hearing: tuning the skips that occur in the soprano and alto parts in the score. Point to the melodic pattern drmfs in the staff notation and ask the singers to

   a. Sing in unison with solfa while inner hearing f on the way up.

   b. Sing in unison with solfa while inner hearing r on the way up.

    c. Repeat steps a and b, singing the same patterns in canon. One group sings as you point, and the other begins to sing two notes later. Your singers will now be singing again in parallel thirds.

B. Staff notation sight-reading from the board:

  1. Soprano part:

    a. "If I sing d, can you still sing r?" (Everyone sings r.)

    b. Point to the staff as only the sopranos sing solfa with hand signs. Repeat if necessary.

    c. Ask individual singers from the soprano section to come up to the board and point to the notes as all of the sopranos sing with solfa and hand signs.

  2. Alto part:

    a. "If I sing d, can you sing t?" (All sing t.)

    b. Point to the staff as only the altos sing with solfa and hand signs. Repeat if necessary.

    c. Ask individual singers from the alto section to come up to the board and point to the notes as all of the altos sing with solfa and hand signs.

  3. Performing in two parts with student leaders:

    a. Sing d and ask the sopranos to sing r and altos to sing t,.

    b. Ask all to sing their own parts with solfa and hand signs.

    c. Have additional students come up to lead the chorus as above.

  4. Reading from the score

    a. "Turn to 'Laughing and Shouting for Joy,' page 5. Can you tell which measure has the same patterns we just practiced on the board?" (Measure 37.)

b. "Sing your own part with solfa as you read your own score." Repeat and rehearse as necessary.

c. "Sing the words from your score as you point to the notes on the staff." If you choose to perform in German, make sure to take time to teach the pronunciation before you do this step.

Notice that in this procedure, I choose to not mention the rhythm. As it is presented here, the singers learn the rhythm by rote as I point. The way it is constructed keeps this teaching strategy purely melodic. If you wish to incorporate rhythm counting because your singers are advanced, and you have the time, you can certainly do so.

Visit the companion website to view a video of this lesson.

REINFORCEMENT THROUGH SIGHT-READING IN TWO PARTS FROM STICK NOTATION

This activity is a bit more challenging since the students are required to know more concepts. Not only are they singing in parallel thirds but also they must know and be able to sing the full diatonic scale, quarter note, single eighth note and rests, and eighth note with two sixteenth notes.

Sound the Trumpet

Henry Purcell

PROCEDURE

d r m f s l s f m r d t, d

A. Tune-up:
   1. Ask your singers to sing the above tone set from the board with solfa and hand signs in the key of D major as you point.
   2. Ask them sing the tone set in a two-part canon in parallel thirds with solfa as you point to improvised melodies in quarter note motion: the sopranos sing as you point, and the altos begin two notes later, performing the same melody.
   3. Ask them to sing the tone set descending from l in a two-part canon as you point.
B. Soprano part:

l   l s s   s s f   f s f m m m r   r m f   m

   1. Ask everyone to sight-read the rhythm with counting or syllables from the stick notation on the board.
   2. Finally, the sopranos sing the solfa as the altos speak the rhythm.
C. Alto part:

f   f m m   m m r   r m r d d d t, t, d r d   d

   1. Ask everyone to sight-read the rhythm with counting or syllables from the stick notation on the board.
   2. Ask the altos to sing the solfa as the sopranos speak the rhythm.
D. Now ask all to sing their own parts, altos and sopranos together, with solfa and hand signs from the board.
E. Reading from the score:
   1. "Take out 'Sound the Trumpet' and look at pages 6 and 7. In which measure do these parts begin?"
   2. Ask everyone to sing their own parts with:
      i. Solfa
      ii. Words

REINFORCEMENT THROUGH SIGHT-READING
TI AND LOW TI

An Invitation

Ralph Vaughn Williams

A. Tune up the entire scale:

1. With solfa and hand signs, ask everyone to sing the E-flat major scale, going up and down from the staff notation on the board as you point.
2. Point to the scale while improvising melodies in rhythms that come from 6/8 time. Everyone sings:
   a. As you point.
   b. After inner hearing patterns that you point to.
   c. Gradually, work in melodies that have the s-d interval, the descending interval of the perfect fifth in the excerpt.
B. Reading the excerpted pattern written on the board:
   1. Point to the first four notes only as everyone sings with solfa and hand signs.
   2. Point to the last five notes as everyone sings with solfa and hand signs.
C. Finally, point to the entire phrase as the choristers sing with solfa and hand signs.
D. Reading from the score:
   1. "Take out 'An Invitation' and turn to page 2. Tell me where you find the pattern from the board in your score."
   2. "Sing the solfa from your own score."
   3. "Sing the words."

SUGGESTED COMPOSITIONS

"Kyrie Eleison" (alto part, measures 85–91)
Franz Schubert
Arranged by Joyce Eilers
For two-part voices and piano
Hal Leonard Publishing
08551023

"All Ye Who Music Love" (Soprano, measures 3–14)
Words by Thomas Oliphant
Music by Baldassare Donato
For two-part and optional piano
Hal Leonard Publishing
08551642

"One Man Shall Mow My Meadow" (measures 9–14)
Arranged by Susan Brumfield
For soprano and alto voices with flute and piano accompaniment
Colla Voce Music
20-96390

LESSON 15
TEACHING THE DOTTED QUARTER NOTE WITH AN EIGHTH NOTE

THE BEST METHOD for teaching dotted quarter note with an eighth note is to use an ostinato. The ostinato should include four eighth notes that occur over the new rhythm, allowing the singers to discover that they can tie three of the eighth notes together to arrive at the dotted quarter note. The fourth eighth note in the ostinato becomes the remaining eighth note in the new rhythm pattern.

Select a song similar to "Chairs to Mend" (presented in the chapter "Building a Foundation") or a choral composition similar to "Sandmännchen" by Brahms. Remember, it is easier to teach new concepts when the singers already know how to sing the melody well.

Sandmännchen

PROCEDURE

A. Discovery by hearing something new:

1. Ask everyone to sing the first two phrases of "Sandmännchen" from memory on text or [lu].

2. "Sometimes you will hear one, two, and no sounds on a beat, and sometimes even one sound that lasts for two beats. Half of you will sing the text and clap with the rhythm. The other half will pat the beat and see if you can hear a new rhythm that is different from what you already know."

3. "Now switch. The half of you who pat the beat should listen carefully and see if you can hear a new rhythm."

4. "Now everyone pat the beat while I sing the words and clap the rhythm, and then tell me which words occur when there is a new rhythm." (*Blüme* and *nikken*.)

5. "Using the words 'long' and 'short,' can you tell me about the new rhythm?" (The first sound is long and the other is short.)

6. "How many beats do these two sounds occur on?" (Two.) If the singers have difficulty answering this question, give them another chance by asking them to pat the beat again as you sing and clap the rhythm of the melody.

B. Ostinato visual:

1. "Clap the rhythm you see on the board over and over as an ostinato as you sing the first phrase only. Listen and look carefully and tell me where the syllables 'Blü' and 'me' occur." (The first and fourth eighth notes.) Write the text under the correct eighth notes.

2. "How many eighth notes does 'Blü' last?" (Three.) "How many eighth notes does 'me' last?" (One.)

3. "Since 'me' is one syllable and has one eighth note with it, the eighth note you see on the board will remain and be part of the new rhythm. But 'Blü' is also one syllable. How many eighth notes do you see above it?" (Three.) "Those three notes will have to change to something different to match the one syllable for 'Blü.'"

4. "What musical device do you know that changes multiple sounds to one longer sound that we can add to the three eighth notes?" (A tie.) Add ties to the first three eighth notes.

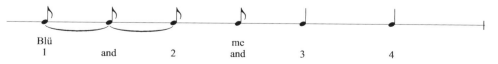

5. "Look at only the first two eighth notes that are tied together. These two sounds have now become how many sounds, now that we've added the tie?" (One.) "What is another way to write one sound on one beat?" (Quarter note.) Change the first two tied eighth notes to a quarter note.

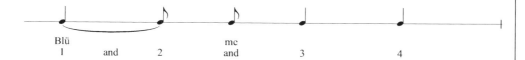

6. "Musicians have another way to simplify and rewrite a quarter note tied to an eighth note. We erase the tie and eighth note and abbreviate them with a dot next to the quarter note." Erase, add a dot, and place parentheses around the words "and 2." The parentheses contain the words of the counting the singers will inner hear while singing and clapping the rhythm. In other words, the word "one" will be sustained for one and a half beats for the duration of the dotted quarter note. After "one," the next words they sing aloud will be the "and" of beat 2, the counting for the eighth note.

C. Naming the new rhythm and practice:
   1. "Listen and watch as I sing, clap, and count the dotted quarter and eighth note." Clap the rhythm while singing counting or rhythm syllables.
   2. "Everyone clap and sing the rhythm."
   3. Practice with smaller groups and solos, and end with everyone together.
D. Reading from the score:
   1. "Take out 'Sandmännchen.' Can you still sing and count the rhythm while reading your own score?"
   2. Ask your singers to sing the words.

REINFORCEMENT THROUGH GUIDED SIGHT-READING

For this activity, select a composition similar to Vaughan Williams's "Spring" from his "Three Children's Songs." The repetition of the dotted quarter/eighth note rhythm in the first two phrases makes it a good choice.

115

Three Children's Songs
I Spring

Frances M. Ferrer

R. Vaughan Williams

Allegretto

Voice

When Sum - mer dons her

Piano

p

dress of green, And__ all the land is bathed in sun;

116

PROCEDURE

A. Before the singers arrive for rehearsal, write the rhythm of the first two phrases of "Spring" on the board in stick notation with the words below, measures 2–6.

B. During the ear development part of your warm-up, practice the rhythms your singers know, including the dotted quarter and eighth note. You can clap and count rhythms that you have written on the board and ask your singers to echo them back. If they are advanced, you can clap the rhythms on the board in random order and ask the singers to identify the one you clapped. They then count and clap it back as you or a student points to the notation on the board. The rhythms that are part of this activity should include rhythms that are similar to the first two phrases of "Spring." For example:

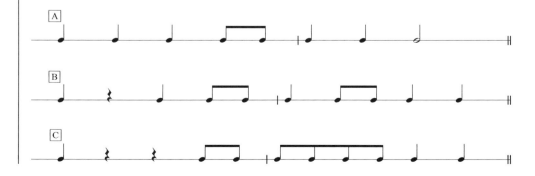

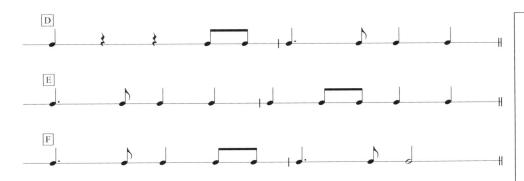

C. After the drill activity above, depending on the skill level of your singers, ask the entire ensemble to sight-read a portion of the "Spring" quotation, or the entire two phrases, with counting and clapping.

D. Practice the reading by having half the ensemble, smaller groups, trios, duets, and solos perform the rhythm. Choristers who are doing particularly well can be asked to go to the board to point to the notation to lead the ensemble's reading.

E. Now ask half the group to clap and count the rhythm as the other half claps and speaks the words written underneath.

F. Switch the groups' roles.

G. Ask everyone to clap and speak the words to the rhythm.

H. Finish by telling the singers to turn to their own scores of "Spring" and ask them to speak the words as they clap the rhythm.

I. Teach them the melody by rote as they quietly tap the rhythm and follow it in their scores as you sing.

J. Ask everyone to tap the rhythm and sing the words.

K. Continue with the rest of your rehearsal with a composition they know well and enjoy singing.

Visit the companion website to download additional sight-reading exercises.

SUGGESTED COMPOSITIONS

"Pie Jesu" from *Requiem* (first four measures)
Gabriel Fauré
Edited and arranged by Doreen Rao
For unison voices and piano
Boosey & Hawkes
OCTB6631

"The Little Birch Tree" (measures 7–12)
Russian folk song
Arranged by Mary Goetze
Unison voices, piano, and recorder or flute

Boosey & Hawkes
OCTB6130

"Gloria" (measures 3–10)
Music by Mary Donnelly
Arranged by George O. Strid
For two-part voices, accompanied
Shawnee Press
E 0368

LESSON 16
TEACHING THE DOTTED EIGHTH NOTE WITH A SIXTEENTH NOTE

IN THIS LESSON, I will demonstrate two ways to teach the dotted eighth note with a sixteenth note. In the first procedure, the singers learn about the rhythm by simply describing it in terms of hearing a longer and a shorter sound. The second procedure leads the singers through discovery of the rhythm on a deeper level of understanding through the use of an ostinato with four sixteenth notes.

Your singers learned from lesson 15 that a shorter note can be tied to a longer one and then abbreviated with a dot to indicate its length. Use the same logic in your approach to teaching the dotted eighth note with a sixteenth note.

"Old Joe Clark," a composition also used in lesson 12, is a good example of repertoire you can use. This time, extract the music from measures 25–32.

Old Joe Clark

Vocal Arrangement by Judy Herrington
Accompaniment by Sara Glick

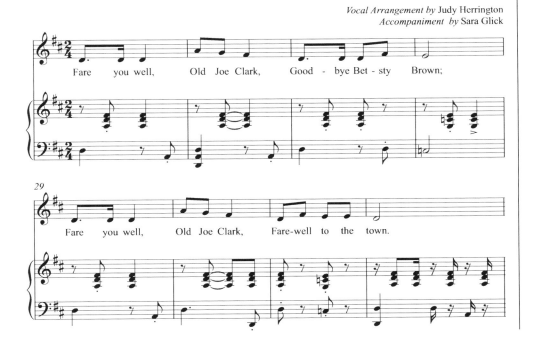

METHOD ONE: DESCRIBING THE RHYTHM

All of your singers should be able to perform this extract from memory with text before beginning this lesson. The singers must also already know the quarter note, two eighth notes, and half note.

PROCEDURE

Prepare the board with the following:

A. Review: "Sometimes we hear one sound on one beat, quarter note, two even sounds on one beat, eighth notes, and one sound lasting for two beats, half note. Pat a beat on your legs and listen carefully as I sing a song you know that has something different. Raise your hand when you hear a different rhythm." Sing the above extract with the words.

B. "What can you tell me about the new rhythm? Does it occur on one or two beats? Make sure you keep the beat on your legs." Sing it again. (Your singers should say it occurs on one beat.)

C. "How many sounds do you hear on the beat when it occurs?" (Two sounds.)

D. "Are they two even sounds?" Sing it again if needed. (No.)

E. "Which of the two sounds is longer, the first or second?" (First.)

F. "Which sound is very short or quick?" (Second.)

G. "We know that two eighth notes are even and occur on one beat." Draw on the board:

H. "We also know that in our new rhythm the first sound is longer. We already know how to make a note longer. How?" (Add a dot.) Draw a dot next to the first eighth note.

I. "And since we know the second sound is quick, or fast, we can add another beam to it." Add a second beam.

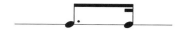

J. "Let's now add this new rhythm to the entire phrase on the board." Write in the rhythm.

K. "Listen as I sing this phrase with the new rhythm name (or counting)."
L. "Everyone sing the rhythm names."
M. "Turn to your score, 'Old Joe Clark,' page 3. Tell me which measures contain our new rhythm." (Measures 25, 27, 29.)
N. "Sing this phrase with rhythm names from your score."
O. "Sing the words."

METHOD TWO: WITH A FOUR-SIXTEENTH-NOTE OSTINATO

As was done in lesson 15 with the dotted quarter note with an eighth note, you can also use an ostinato to derive the dotted eighth note with a sixteenth note. This time, instead of eighth notes in the ostinato, you will have to use sixteenth notes. Gradually morph the rhythm until you arrive at dotted eighth note and a sixteenth note. This is probably a more effective way to teach this combination of rhythms, because the students will discover that the dotted eighth note consists of three sixteenth notes, and therefore they will have a deeper understanding of the rhythm.

In this procedure, the singers discover the new rhythm as they did in steps A–F of the previous procedure.

PROCEDURE

Suggested ostinato:

A. Ask your singers to clap the sixteenth note ostinato and notice where the words fall on the four sixteenths. ("Fare" occurs on the first note and "you" on the last.) Write the words underneath.

Fare   you

121

B. "What can we add to the first three sixteenth notes to change them into one sound?" (Ties.) Draw ties.

Fare you

C. "What is another way to write two sixteenth notes that are tied together?" (Eighth note.) Add the eighth note.

Fare you

D. "Tell me how we can abbreviate the tied sixteenth note and write the rhythm another way. We learned how to do this when we learned another rhythm that you know." (Change it to a dot.) Erase the tied eighth note and draw a dot.

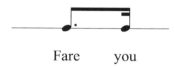

Fare you

E. Continue with steps J–O from the previous procedure.

REMINDER

As you continue with your rehearsal, make sure that you take any opportunity to reinforce this new concept by asking your singers to find and identify the rhythms in other compositions.

REINFORCEMENT THROUGH GUIDED SIGHT-READING

One of the best ways to practice a rhythmic concept is to sight-read it in another piece of music. Set up your singers for success by beginning with one of the rhythmic reinforcement activities in the appendix. The more you prepare your singers with the skills they need for the discovery process, the better they will feel about the adventure of music reading.

Find in your repertoire a composition similar to Shirley W. McRae's arrangement of "Goin' to Boston" that prominently features the dotted eighth note with a sixteenth note.

Goin' to Boston

American Folk Song
Arranged by
Shirley W. McRae

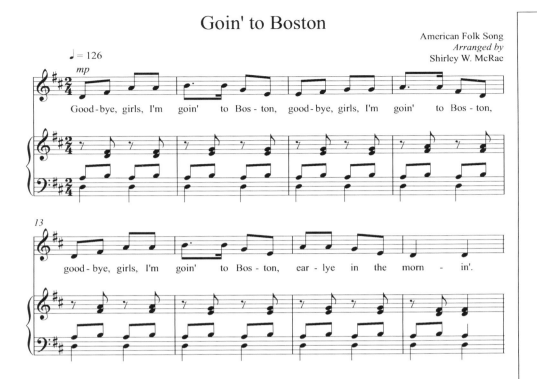

PROCEDURE

A. Practice/warm-up activity: draw the following eight rhythms from "Old Joe Clark" (or similar rhythms from another composition that you used to teach the dotted eighth note with a sixteenth note) on cards, or print them out from the companion website, and tape them to the board in random order before rehearsal. The goal for your singers will be to arrange the cards in the correct order and sing the rhythm counting for the song.

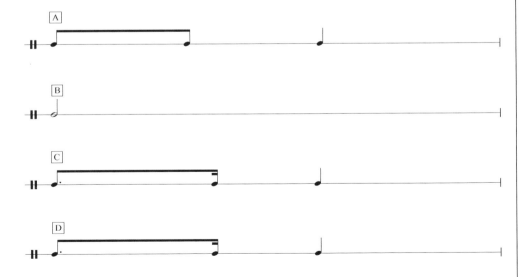

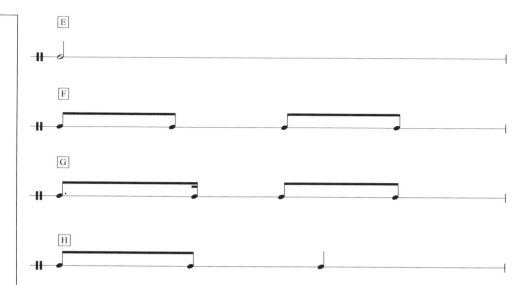

1. "Sing the words and clap the rhythm of 'Old Joe Clark.'"
2. "Sing the rhythm counting [or names] and clap for the same melody."
3. "Look at the eight cards on the board. Let's work together to rearrange them so they are in the correct order for 'Old Joe Clark.'" Ask your singers to say which one goes first, or ask individuals to place single cards in the correct order until all the cards are arranged. Help the singers by repeating the singing of the rhythm, counting for the entire excerpt as needed.
4. "Sing the song from the beginning with clapping and counting of the rhythm to check if our work is correct." You, or another singer, should point to the rhythm to guide the ensemble's reading.

B. Sight-reading the rhythm of "Goin' to Boston":
1. Place cards F and G in a prominent place on the board and say, "Now clap and speak the rhythm of the remaining two cards." Everyone claps and speaks.
2. "Now repeat those two cards three times without stopping."
3. "Take out 'Goin' to Boston.' Look at the first page of music and tell me in which measure you find the rhythm from the board?" (Measure 9.)
4. "Say the rhythm names as you point to the notes in your own score." Make sure your singers are all reading the notes and following them on the page. Help those who need it by repeating this step and showing them how to follow the notation.
5. "Turn the page. Are the next four measures exactly the same as the first page?" (No.)
6. "Try clapping and saying the counting for this new phrase."
7. "Go back to the first page. Point and say the counting for both phrases." Repeat this step as needed until everyone is counting and following correctly.

8. "Sopranos, say the rhythm names as the altos speak the words printed underneath the staff to the same rhythm. Everyone should still point to the notes on the staff."

9. "Switch. Altos, say the rhythm names; sopranos, say the words to the rhythm."

10. "Everyone speak the words underneath the rhythm on the staff."

11. Repeat this with smaller groups and even soloists. This practice of the activity in smaller groups allows you to help correct any mistakes. End with everyone performing together.

12. Teach the melody by rote. "Echo me after I sing the words to the melody for the song."

13. Continue with the rest of the rehearsal.

Visit the companion website to download the rhythm cards for "Old Joe Clark."

Notice that you taught the melody by rote. The reason for this is that the focus of the Lesson was to work on rhythm. Most likely, the rhythm work took a bit of time. Sight-singing the melody in the same rehearsal would probably be too much—your singers will be ready to move on. Be careful to balance the time and concentration that the reading skills take with the attention span and patience of your singers.

Visit the companion website to download additional sight-reading exercises.

SUGGESTED COMPOSITIONS

"Kyrie Eleison" (alto part, measures 85–91)
Franz Schubert
Arranged by Joyce Eilers
For two-part voices and piano
Hal Leonard Publishing
08551023

"Our Gallant Ship" (rhythm is prominent throughout the melody)
Susan Brumfield
For two soprano voices and alto voice with horn and piano
Colla Voce Music
20-96100

"Shady Grove" (with "The Cuckoo") (rhythm prominent throughout)
Traditional folk songs
Arranged by Nancy Boone Allsbrook and Glenda Goodin
Boosey & Hawkes
48020941

LESSON 17
TEACHING LOW SOL

YOUR SINGERS HAVE ALREADY learned to expand the tone set both higher and lower. Hearing s, flows quite easily when we relate it to l,.

Look for a musical passage in your repertoire that places l, and s, next to each other as neighbor tones, so your singers will be able to hear there is a new sound below l,. The melody of treble part II in measure 66 of "American Rhapsody" is a good example of the perfect pitch pattern.

American Folk Rhapsody

PROCEDURE

Reminder: If you are to use the above excerpt to teach a new concept, the choristers should know how to sing the excerpt well with text. Prepare the board with the following before the singers arrive for rehearsal:

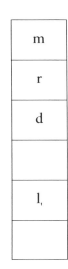

A. Begin with a melodic practice activity in which the singers practice the known tone set: l, drm s. For example,

   1. Choristers echo-sing patterns after you from the tone ladder:
      a. drmrdl,d
      b. mrdl,d
      c. drmmdl,
      d. l,dl,drrm
      e. mddl,d

   2. Repeat the above or similar patterns while pointing to the staff notation.

B. "Listen carefully as I sing a short phrase on [lu] from a composition you already know. Raise your hands when you hear a sound that is different from l, drm. The melody begins on m." If the choristers do not raise their hands at the correct moment, it indicates they need more practice with the known tone set. Slow down and reinforce what they know with some of the suggested melodic reinforcement activities in the appendix.

C. "Is the new sound higher or lower?" (Lower). Sing the excerpt again if they need help answering this question.

D. "Yes, it is a sound that is below low l. After I sing the words again, can you tell if it is a step or a skip lower than l,? In other words, is it close or far below l?" (Step lower/close.)

E. "You already know the name of this sound. What is a step lower than l?" (s).

F. "Since this tone is lower than d we call it low so and add it to the tone ladder." Draw s, on the bottom, empty space of the tone ladder.

G. Pointing to the notation of the excerpt: "If d is on the first space, and l, on the space below the staff, where will we write the new sound on the staff?" (The ledger line below the staff.) (This is the time to teach the concept of the ledger line if you have not already done so. Define it as added lines and spaces to create higher and lower notes to the staff.) Draw the note s, on the staff.

H. "Listen and watch as I sing the solfa and show the hand sign for s,." Make sure you show the hand sign lower than the sign for l,. Show the hand signs underneath each note in the staff notation on the board to guide the singers' reading.

I. "Everyone sing solfa and show hand signs."

J. Continue practicing the new concept with smaller groups and soloists, ending with everyone. Consider asking an individual to go to the board to point to the notes and lead the group.

K. "Turn to page 12 of 'American Rhapsody.' Tell me where you find the pattern we have been practicing on the board." (Measure 66 in the treble 2 part.)

L. "Point to the notes in your own score and sing the solfa." As conductor/teacher, make sure that you observe and help any singers who need help following the notes in the score. Remember that actual music reading from the score is the point here, and some beginning singers will need assistance.

M. "Sing the words."

N. Continue with the rest of your rehearsal. Make sure you find other places where s, is found and reinforce it in the same rehearsal. This repetition will ensure that the singers will remember the new concept for the next rehearsal.

REINFORCEMENT THROUGH GUIDED SIGHT-READING

I Bought Me A Cat

Traditional
Arranged by Linda Steen Spevacek

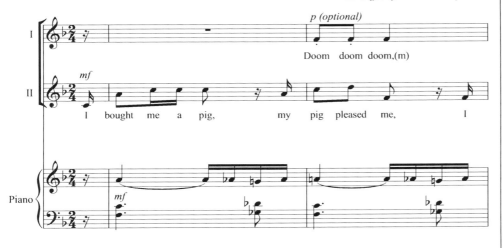

Concepts the singers must already know before learning this strategy:

1. dt₁l₁s₁
2. Ledger line for middle C
3. Quarter note and two eighth notes
4. Tie

PROCEDURE

A. Review staff notation:

129

1. Sing solfa with hand signs: d t₁ l₁ s₁ d s₁ d
2. Ask your singers to echo with hand signs.
3. Use d s₁ d as a vocalise with your singers:
   a. Everyone sings solfa, moving the pattern up and down by half steps.
   b. End in F major.

B. Pattern from "I Bought Me a Cat": read from staff notation on the board.

1. Ask half of the singers to clap and speak rhythm names while the other half sings solfa and shows hand signs.
2. Switch the roles of the two groups.

C. Say to your singers: "Turn to your score, page 5. Where do you find this pattern from the board in your score?" (Beginning in measure 43.)

D. Singing from the score:
1. Ask everyone to sing solfa.
2. All sing the letter names.
3. Everyone sings rhythm names.
4. Sing the alto part with the words as all sing the soprano with solfa.
5. Altos sing their part with the words as sopranos sing with:
   a. Solfa
   b. The words

ADDITIONAL REINFORCEMENT: DERIVING AND SINGING THE SOLFA OF A KNOWN MELODY

A composition similar to the following arrangement of "Chatter with the Angels" is a good choice to reinforce s₁. The objective of the following activity is to have the singers sing the well-known melody with solfa without looking at the score notation. Prepare them with a brief echo activity that includes the tone set s₁ l₁ d r m. This preparation will ensure that the singers will be more successful in completing the objective. The choristers must know the melody very well before beginning an activity like this.

Chatter with the Angels

Spiritual
arranged by
Charles Collins

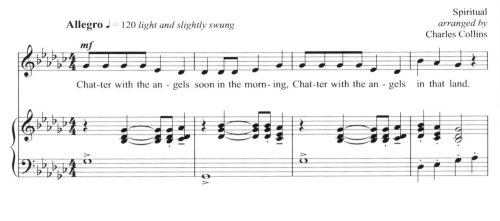

PROCEDURE

A. Echo activity:

1. Conductor sings the following, or similar patterns, with solfa and hand signs in the key of G-flat major, and the choristers sing them back with solfa and hand signs.

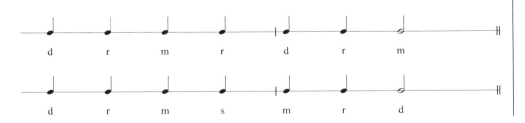

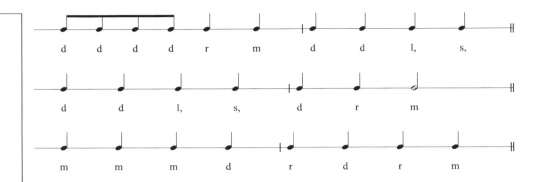

d   d   d   d   r   m   d   d   l,   s,

d   d   l,   s,   d   r   m

m   m   m   d   r   d   r   m

2. Repeat the same patterns as you sings them on [lu] as the choristers sing back with solfa and hand signs.

B. Singing "Chatter with the Angels":

1. Ask the choristers to sing the words of "Chatter with the Angels" without any help from you or the piano.

2. Say to the singers, "If the melody of 'Chatter with the Angels' begins on d, can you sing the solfa and hand signs for the melody after I sing the words?" Sing only two measures at a time as you make your way through the entire excerpt.

3. "Now, let's have the altos sing the words as I did while the sopranos echo them by singing the melody with solfa and hand signs."

4. "Now switch."

5. "Now try to sing the entire melody with solfa and hand signs."

6. "Sing the words as you take out your scores for 'Chatter with the Angels.'"

7. Since this was a heavy concentration activity, it is a good idea to let them sing as much of the piece they know without rehearsing it in too much detail. Remember to keep these procedures light, fun, and short.

SUGGESTED COMPOSITIONS

"Little David, Play on Your Harp" (soprano part, measures 3–7)
Spiritual
Arranged by Emily Crocker
Jenson Publications
4712301

"Hush!" (part I1, measures 7–14)
Traditional spiritual and carols
Arranged by Sally K. Albrecht
For two-part voices and piano
Alfred Publishing
19297

LESSON 18
TEACHING THE MINOR SCALE

NOW THAT YOUR SINGERS know l₁, t₁, and f, the natural minor is easy to teach. They know the order of the whole and half steps that occur with the corresponding solfa in the major scale, using d as the tonic. It will be logical for them to understand and perform the minor scale when they sing melodies that end on l. When singing the entire minor scale with solfa—ltdrmfsl—the whole and half steps are where they need to be, between td and mf.

As always, teach this new concept by using repertoire your singers already know. "The Little Birch Tree" is a good example of the type of composition you can use. It is a good choice since l, is approached by descending from tones the singers already know: mrd and t.

The Little Birch Tree

Russian Folk Song
Arranged by Mary Goetze

PROCEDURE

Write the following on the board before rehearsal begins:

A. Begin with an echo activity from the tone ladder that tunes up some of the melodic pattern in "The Little Birch Tree." Ask your singers to perform with solfa and hand signs after you sing simple patterns with solfa and hand signs. Make the exercise more challenging by asking them to echo you after you sing on [lu] with hand signs, and finally only [lu] with no signs. If your singers are advanced, you can make this activity even more challenging if you conclude with only showing the hand signs. For example:

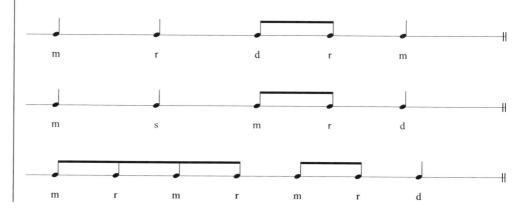

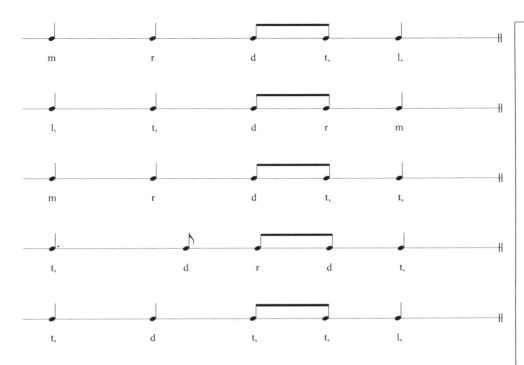

m   r   d   t,   l,

l,   t,   d   r   m

m   r   d   t,   t,

t,   d   r   d   t,

t,   d   t,   t,   l,

B. Point to the staff notation of the "Little Birch Tree" excerpt and review the solfa placement on the staff: d is on the second line; r on the second space; m the third line; and so on.

C. Ask your singers to read the entire melody with solfa and hand signs as you point to the staff.

D. Ask them which solfa name they ended on (l.)

E. Ask them if that tone sounds like a resting tone, that is, identify whether or not the song sounds like it is finished. (Yes.)

F. Review that when melodies end on d, the scale is major.

G. Explain to your singers that when melodies end on l, it is the scale is minor.

H. Reinforce this new concept by asking them to sing "The Little Birch Tree" again. Stress that the song is composed in the minor scale.

I. If they know letter names, you can ask them the name of the final note. Tell them that when E equals l and the music ends on this note, then the composition is in E minor.

APPLICATION OF MINOR: TEACHING RELATIVE MAJOR AND MINOR

Now that your singers know they can end on l while singing in minor, you can now show them the relationship between major and relative minor. For example, ask them to sing "The Little Birch Tree" with solfa. Ask them which letter name is called d, the note for the beginning of the major scale. They should respond that G is d. You can now point out that G major and E minor share the

135

same key signature, and are related: E minor is the relative minor of G major, and G major is the relative major of E minor.

REINFORCEMENT THROUGH GUIDED SIGHT-READING

Your singers are now ready to apply the minor scale to echo-singing and tone-ladder and staff activities, including sight-reading and other melodic reinforcement exercises (see appendix). For example, Benjamin Britten's composition "Old Abram Brown," from his collection of songs "Friday Afternoons," is a good piece for practicing l-based solfa.

Old Abram Brown

From "Tom Tiddler's Ground"
by Walter de la Mare

Music by
Benjamin Britten

PROCEDURE

Write the following on the board before rehearsal:

A. Review the names of the solfa on the staff notation. Ask your singers if the melody will be in major or minor if they end on l. (Minor.) Point to simple melodic patterns similar to those in the melody of "Old Abram Brown," in order to tune up the difficulties in the sight-reading. Ask your singers to perform with solfa and hand signs when you point to the staff and

    1. Sing solfa.

    2. Sing [lu].

    3. Only point.

These melodic patterns can include the following:

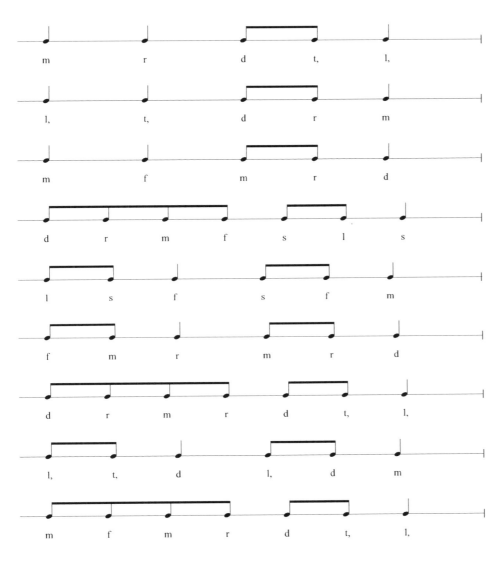

B. If your singers are advanced, you should ask them to sight-sing, using solfa and hand signs, the melody of "Old Abram Brown" from their own scores. If they are less experienced, you can guide their sight-singing from staff notation of the melody on the board. Separate the melody into shorter motifs according to their ability. For example, the simplest way to read might be:

1. Ask the singers to read all the individual motifs as you point to the notation on the board.
2. Next ask them to sing all of them together without stopping as you point to the notation on the board.
3. Now ask them to sing the solfa from their own scores as they point to the notes.
4. Finish by asking everyone to sing the lyrics of the song from their scores.

ADDITIONAL EXAMPLE OF REPERTOIRE FOR MINOR

Try applying similar activities that you explored above to the teaching of "A Daffodil, Too!" by B. Wayne Bisbee. Excerpt the melody from the B section of the composition where "Daisy" begins, measure 24.

Look at the structure of the melody and discover the difficult melodic patterns that you can tune up on the tone ladder, or staff notation, before asking the singers to read the entire melody. These patterns should include:

mmdrd
mml,
l,l,mmd
drmsm
mlsf
fr
smd
l,dm
mrdt,l,

A Daffodil, Too!

Peggy Leavitt

B. Wayne Bisbee

139

Sight-read the melody in its entirety, or in shorter motifs, according to your singers' ability level. Finally, end by asking the singers to perform from their own scores.

SUGGESTED COMPOSITIONS

"With the Earth, I Am One" (part I, measures 5–12)
Judith Herrington
For two-part voices, piano, and cello
Hal Leonard Corporation
08752511

"The Angel Gabriel" (measures 11–26)
Basque carol
Arranged by John Raymond Howell
Boosey & Hawkes
OCT. 6256

LESSON 19
LIEBESLIEDER WALZER, BY JOHANNES BRAHMS

THE STRATEGIES PROVIDED here are musically more advanced. It is ideal to ask the singers to read the patterns with solfa while only viewing the staff notation on the board and from their scores if they have good fluency in solfa. However, if the level of the group is not advanced, then the solfa names can be copied underneath the notation.

Johannes Brahms intended his *Liebeslieder Walzer,* op. 52, to be performed by a small, intimate ensemble suitable for salon recitals. They were so popular during his lifetime that he arranged them for piano solo and composed a second set, the *Neue Liebeslieder,* op. 65. Even though they were meant for a small group of singers, they also sound wonderful with larger ensembles.

Performing the entire set is preferable if you have the time. However, if you are looking for a shorter set, I recommend the following excerpts with a combination of performances from the entire ensemble, duets, and even solos. This worked well for me when I chose to perform them some years ago with the University Chorus at San Francisco State University.

"Am Donaustrande," no. 9
"O wie sanft die Quelle sich," no. 10
"Nein, es ist nicht auszukommen," no. 11
"Schlosser auf, und mache Schlösser," no. 12
"Vögelein durchrauscht die Luft," no. 13
"Sieh, wie ist die Welle klar," no. 14
"Nachtigall, sie singt so schön," no. 15
"Nicht wandle, mein Licht," no. 17
"Zum Schluss," from *Neue Liebeslieder,* op. 65

Adding "Zum Schluss" from the second set of Brahms's waltzes, *Neue Liebeslieder,* op. 65, is effective because this movement contains the end of the poetry and brings the drama of the love songs to finality: "zum schluss" means "in conclusion."

PROCEDURE FOR SIGHT-READING THE ALTO PART

A. Tune-up:
1. All sing the following three patterns with solfa and hand signs from the board as you first point to the tone ladder. Once they are able to sing them well, you should then point to the patterns in staff notation on the board as they sing with sofa and hand signs. Practicing these patterns in this way makes the sight-reading easier.

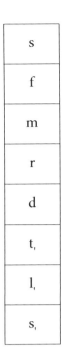

B. Sight-reading the alto part:

1. Ask the singers to perform the following three motifs individually from the board with solfa as you point:

2. Ask the singers to perform all three motifs together without stopping.

C. Score:

1. Immediately ask the singers to perform the solfa from their own scores as they read the alto part, measures 3–17. If needed, sing only one motif at a time before stringing them together.

2. Sing the words from their own scores.

Vögelein durchraust die Luft

Johannes Brahms

144

PROCEDURE FOR SIGHT-READING THE SOPRANO AND ALTO

A. Tune-up:

1. Sing a scale warm-up exercise, similar to the previous procedure, in the key of A-flat major, making sure that s, is practiced.

2. Singers echo the following patterns from staff notation written on the board after you points to the notation and sings with solfa. The impor-

tant sounds and accompanying notes the singers should practice and place in their ears and eyes are the tonic and dominant seventh chords that make up so much of the first half of this movement.

3. You gradually begin to point to patterns on the board that lead to the leaps of the motifs that exist in the score.

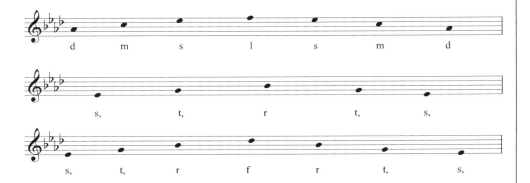

B. Score application:
1. The singers read the melody from their scores by singing solfa in slow quarter note motion.
2. You sing the correct rhythm with solfa, and all echo-sing.
3. All echo the solfa in the correct rhythm.

PROCEDURE FOR TEACHING HARMONIC MINOR

The easiest of strategies can consist of simply singing the tone set, or scale, of a composition. More developed lessons can introduce new, advanced musical concepts connected to the scale of a piece of music. Using "Schlosser auf, und mache Schlösser," try teaching natural and harmonic minor scales.

Schlösser, auf

Johannes Brahms

A. Tune-up:
1. All sing an E-flat major scale from the board with solfa:

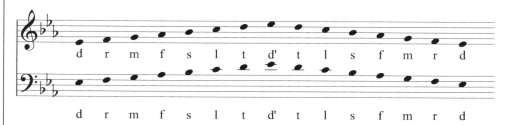

2. All sing from d descending to l₁:

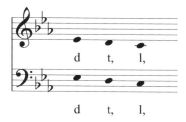

3. All immediately sing a C-natural minor scale from the board as you point to the staff notation. (You name the scale "natural minor.")

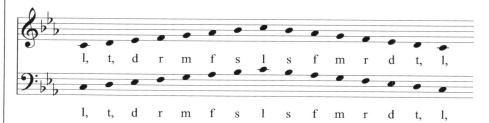

B. Naming the harmonic minor scale:
1. "What type of step is there between s and l?" (Whole step.)
2. "Here's how we make it a half step, like t to d in the major scale." (You add a B-natural to the staff notation, name it as si, and sing the scale with si instead of s.) It will be even more helpful to provide a keyboard visual so your singers can observe the half step between the notes B and C.

3. "This is the harmonic minor scale."
4. The singers echo the scale with solfa after you.

C. Score: At this point it will be too much for a chorus with beginning skills to sight-sing melodies using solfa for the minor scale. However, they should learn to associate the sound with staff notation. To this end, this procedure has now taught the singers how to recognize what the scale looks and sounds like on the staff. To apply this teaching, ask your ensemble to look at the beginning of "Schlosser auf, und mache Schlösser" and identify the key and the scale. Ask them to identify and tell which note indicates that the tone set is in C harmonic minor (B-natural) and in which voice it occurs. (Alto.)

Reinforce harmonic minor with echo-singing activities or warm-up vocalises and through analysis of other compositions in your repertoire that happen to be in minor keys.

ADVANCED PROCEDURE WITH MODULATION

O, wie sanft die Quelle

In this procedure the singers will learn the melodic structure of "O wie sanft die Quelle," measures 11–21, call and response, as well as the movement's individual motifs through more advanced warm-up reading exercises. The tool I use is stick notation from the board. Of course, if your ensemble's skills are advanced you can teach them directly from the notation in the score.

PROCEDURE

    A. All sing a G major scale exercise to tune up the tone set for the singers' ears.

    B. Stick notation:

       1. Alto part:

         a. From stick notation on the board, the singers echo after you or sight-sing with solfa according to their skill level.

         b. All write solfa for the alto part, measures 15–21, in their scores.

         c. All sing the alto part from the score with solfa.

       2. Bass part:

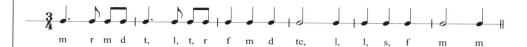

         a. All echo-sing or sight-sing the solfa after you sing the excerpt.

         b. "What is the name of the solfa, the note in this exercise that is different from the previous melody?" (te).

         c. "Does this sound higher or lower than ti?" (Lower.)

         d. Singers sing from the board as you point.

         e. Singers write the solfa in the bass part beginning in measure 16.

         f. All sing from the score with solfa.

       3. All sing from the score in two parts with women singing the alto beginning in measure 15 and the men singing the bass beginning in measure 16 from their own scores.

This is probably enough for one rehearsal. The key to these strategies is to keep them short and to the point. Remember, there is a lot of repertoire to cover to get ready for the concert!

    A more advanced teaching segment introduces modulation, a change of keys, and a change of d. In the first example, when the singers get to the fourth measure in the key of C major, s (or G) now becomes d in the key of G major.

When the singers perform this modulation they will sing the downbeat of the fourth measure twice. The first time they sing the pitch G two times, first as s and then repeating as d. Once they master the key change they can then immediately sing this beat once as d in G major.

PROCEDURE

A. Soprano part:

1. All echo the melody with solfa after you. Sing the pivot tone as s and immediately repeat it, calling it d. This change of solfa will eliminate any chromatic solfa for the second half of the melody.
2. Singers write the solfa in the soprano part beginning in measure 12 in their scores.
3. All sing the pattern with solfa from their scores.

B. Tenor part: Use the same process as above, but now apply it to the tenor part in measure 11.

Now the entire section of music, measures 11–21, is ready to be sung with solfa, and the major themes for this movement have now been taught and sung by the chorus.

If your ensemble has a less advanced ability level, and a shorter attention span, I recommend teaching the themes above by spreading them over two or three rehearsals. The last two themes will take a bit more time since they involve modulation and are more difficult.

Of course, if your ensemble's skills are advanced you can teach these themes directly from the score.

You can see that this advanced level of instruction takes a bit of analysis on your part. But isn't this part of our score preparation? I believe it should be. The better we as conductors know these types of melodic and harmonic turns, the better we know the composer's intent. The knowledge gained from our score study and analysis will make us more adept at teaching the score to our singers, and our singers will get to the music more quickly as a result of their new and developing music literacy skills.

LESSON 20
EAR TRAINING AND ADVANCED THEORY IN THE REHEARSAL

ONCE A MUSICAL CONCEPT, melodic and rhythmic, has been introduced to the ensemble, it never goes away. Rather, it is moved into practice and reinforcement activities that I suggest earlier in this text. Additional practice can involve activities that focus on music theory concepts as well as ear training. A well-trained ear is crucial to ensembles that perform with the highest levels of musicianship and nuance.

The following strategies are ones I taught to the San Francisco Symphony Chorus as assistant director in the fall of 2010. They were developed with the director's goals for the chorus in mind. Obviously, this ensemble has a high level of skills. My point is that no matter what the singers' level is, you can always find something to review or new concepts to introduce.

THE TRIAD: ROOT, THIRD, OR FIFTH?

One of the interesting aspects of music is the living, active nature of melodic and harmonic tuning. A single note on the staff often becomes higher or lower in pitch on the basis of its melodic and harmonic context. And the piano, which is in tempered tuning, is out of tune with perfect, natural acoustical tuning. When accompanied by the piano, we as singers have learned out-of-tune singing in order to accommodate and match the piano. The major third is much too high, and the major second and minor thirds are too low. When we sing independently of the piano we should sing differently. And when we become aware of our places in harmony, we can begin to make subtle shifts in pitch that can often dramatically change the sound of a chord. The following instruction and ear training activities will help singers discover their places in a triad. Divide the ear training over several rehearsals.

    A. There are three parts to a triad: root, third, and fifth.
       1. Ask the singers to echo you as you hum a major triad up and down.
       2. Have all sing a major triad with solfa: dmsmd.

B. Function of the tones:

    1. The root of the triad can be a place of tremendous rest. And in terms of balance of the chord, the root should be the most prominent tone to the listener.

    2. The third of the chord provides the "color" and makes it either major or minor. In terms of balance, it should be dynamically prominent.

    3. The fifth fills out the chord and provides a bit of harmonic stability; the fifth should sound softer than the other tones.

C. Ear training:

    1. Root, third, or fifth?

        a. Play or sing various root tones and have all hum major or minor triads up and down.

        b. The singers hum a given pitch played from the piano and then try to descend to the root of a chord the director plays on the piano. The singers then identify whether the initial tone was the third or the fifth. For example:

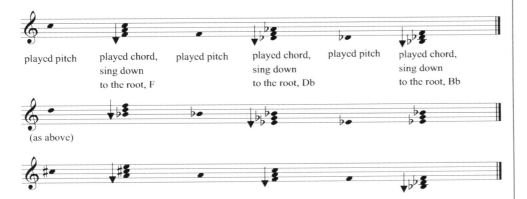

    2. Tuning:

        a. Pitch is like white light. White light is actually made of many colors (red, orange, yellow, green, blue, indigo, violet), and a single pitch is made up of many pitches found in the overtone series.

        b. Singers are in tune when they match the pitch or pitches in another tone's specific set of overtone series.

        c. Tuning the perfect fifth of the triad: play the lowest given pitch and have the singers hum or sing solfa up through the scale until they reach the fifth of the chord. They should sing slowly and softly and listen carefully to each note and compare it to the fundamental pitch you play on the piano to make sure that they are in tune. Since the pitch on the piano decays quickly on the piano, you repeat the pitch as needed.

Major: root   fifth   Major: root   fifth   minor: root   fifth

b. Demonstrate for the singers what the perfect fifth sounds like when it is out of tune. Play the root on the piano and bend the fifth slightly higher and lower than the in-tune fifth. There is strong dissonance!

c. Tuning the major and minor thirds of the triad: divide your ensemble into three parts. Two of the parts will build a perfect fifth. Ask the remaining section to sing up through the scale slowly to either a major or minor third. They should hum or sing solfa. The goal in this ear training activity is to listen and tune to the other sections of the ensemble. Sing the following a cappella:

Make sure that you immediately find places to apply the above exercises in the scores that your ensemble is preparing.

INTERVAL TRAINING

Once your ensemble knows how to perform the entire major scale, you can introduce intervals up and down from the tonic of the scale.

A. All sing a D major scale up and down with solfa as you play D and A on the piano as a perfect fifth drone, repeating as needed as the sound decays.

B. Sing the scale again with d between each tone as the singers ascend, and d' between each tone as they descend:

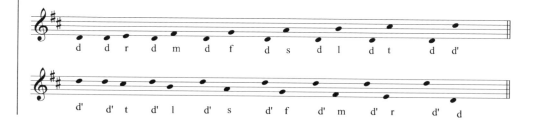

C. After the singers are able to sing the scale fluently with d and d' between each note of the scale, you can then introduce and sing the interval names:

> dr major second, dm major third, df perfect fourth, and so on.
>
> d't minor second, d'l minor third, d's perfect fourth, and so on.

D. Apply this new skill by finding places in the scores the ensemble is preparing to isolate several intervals and have the singers sing them with solfa.

E. Tell the singers to practice these exercises on their own so they eventually have them memorized.

F. For advanced singers, ask them to sing the exercise up and down from r, from m, and so on, instead of d.

MINOR SCALES: A MAJOR DEAL!

You can introduce or practice the minor scale by teaching it on the basis of the information the singers in your ensemble already know, specifically, the major scale. Prepare the board with the first three staves below and make alterations as they occur with the harmonic and melodic scales if you decide to teach them all at once.

A. Introduction

1. All sing F major scale up and down with solfa.

2. Transition by singing through the scale from d down to l.

3. All sing a scale up and down from l, to l. Name this scale as the natural minor scale.

Using l as a tonic is entirely up to you. However, as you can see from the above activity, it is a natural flow out of the major scale, the information your ensemble already knows. And the whole and half steps are already in place. If you want to use d as the tonic, you can immediately repeat the scale with a few modifications of the solfa:

d   r   me   f   s   le   te   d'   te   le   s   f   me   r   d

4. Harmonic minor:
   a. You sing the scale on [lu] with the seventh tone raised, in this case, C-sharp, and ask the singers to raise their hands when they hear a different tone.
   b. Ask the singers how the seventh tone was different: Was it higher or lower? (Higher.)
   c. Ask the singers what music symbol should be added. (Sharp.)
   d. You add C-sharp and sing the scale up and down with solfa, followed by the ensemble. Name the scale the harmonic minor scale.
   e. All sing the scale with solfa.

l,   t,   d   r   m   f   si   l   si   f   m   r   d   t,   l,
d   r   me   f   s   le   t   d'   t   le   s   f   me   r   d

5. Melodic minor:
   a. You sing the scale up and down with raised sixth and seventh tones and ask the singers to raise their hands when they hear something different. (There is a common definition of this scale that has the sixth and seventh scale degrees raised while ascending and lowered descending. This is a poor definition, since the tones are often raised while descending, especially in baroque style. We should define the harmonic minor scale to our singers as a minor scale with raised sixth and seventh scale degrees.) Ask them which tone was different, and how? (Sixth, higher.)
   b. Ask the singers which music symbol will make B-flat higher. (Natural.)
   c. You add B-natural and sing the scale with the new solfa.
   d. All sing the scale with solfa.

l,   t,   d   r   m   fi   si   l   si   fi   m   r   d   t,   l,
d   r   me   f   s   l   t   d'   t   l   s   f   me   r   d

I taught all three scales to the San Francisco Symphony Chorus in one rehearsal. Despite the length of this lesson plan, it actually moves quite quickly. And since we were working on Mozart's *Requiem* I immediately reinforced each minor scale by finding short examples of all three scales in the score and asked the entire chorus to sing the excerpts with solfa. It is always a good idea to show immediate application to the learning and performance of repertoire.

APPENDIX
PRACTICE AND REINFORCEMENT ACTIVITIES FOR MELODY AND RHYTHM

REINFORCEMENT ACTIVITIES PRACTICE musical concepts. Spend several rehearsals practicing what is new by incorporating the following suggested activities before moving into subsequent lessons. Beginners need a lot of repetition! You should incorporate these activities in the warm-up portion of each rehearsal when the energy of the ensemble is fresh. It is also possible to place them in the middle of a rehearsal as a way to break up the intense rehearsing of repertoire.

MELODY

Activities that reinforce melody include:

A. Ask the choristers to echo-sing melodic patterns of the known tone set with solfa and hand signs. Progress from simple to more difficult. The conductor:
  1. Sings solfa and shows hand signs.
  2. Sings [lu] and shows hand signs.
  3. Sings only [lu] with no hand signs.
  4. Shows only hand signs and does not sing.
B. Use a tone ladder on the board. Ask everyone to sing patterns with solfa and hand signs. (Only add the tones your singers know to the ladder.)

r'
d'
t
l
s
f
m
r
d
t,

1. First, ask the choristers to sing as you point.

2. After you point to four beat patterns: the singers inner hear and then sing back by memory. **Note:** Advanced singers can take your place as conductors to lead the ensemble in the above activities. Ask your singers to derive the solfa of other well-known songs or patterns in your repertoire, and perform those excerpts with hand signs.

C. Create multiple cards with solfa of short motifs of a known melody and mix them up on the board. Ask the singers to arrange them in the correct order and perform the melody with solfa and hand signs.

D. The above activities can be reinforced with the methods below:

1. Ask everyone to sing back letter names.

2. Half of the ensemble sings solfa and the other half of the singers perform with letter names.

E. Teach the concept of open (melodies not ending on d in major and l in minor, also known as a musical question) and closed (melodies ending on d or l, also known as a musical answer) cadences. Sing a melody with an open cadence, or the musical question:

drmrdrm

Then your singers sing the melody with a closed cadence, or the musical answer, with solfa and/or letter names:

drmrdrd

F. After you sing, ask your singers to write down simple dictations after you sing patterns with

1. Solfa

2. Letter names

3. [lu]

4. After you play patterns on the piano or another instrument

G. Ask your singers to analyze and find known melodic patterns in a composition from the ensemble's repertoire.

H. Create a melodic strategy: the singers sight-read melodies with the known solfa in the ensemble's current repertoire.

I. Add rhythm on the staffs of melodies your singers know and read them from the choral score with both solfa and rhythm names/counting.

J. Once your singers know how to sing the solfa well for a phrase or entire song, ask them to inner hear and show all the hand signs for one or more of the tones. Repeat the exercise until they can inner hear the entire melody with hand signs.

K. Ask your singers to inner hear well-known music while showing the hand signs and thinking of the melody with solfa. On cue, perhaps when they hear you strike a drum, ask them to sing aloud until they hear the drum again, which will signal them to inner hear again. You signal them to switch back and forth several times, depending on the length of the music.

L. Ask your singers to improvise four- or eight-beat melodies using the solfa they know.

RHYTHM

As you did with the melodic reinforcement activities, make sure to incorporate the practice of rhythmic skills as well during the "ear" portion of your warm-up. If you have time, do both rhythm and melody. If not, alternate them in your rehearsals.

Your singers should always count or say rhythm syllables.

A. After you clap simple four-beat patterns, ask your singers to echo you by clapping and counting. Progress from easy to more difficult:
    1. You clap and count.
    2. You clap only.
B. Ask your singers to perform known musical phrases while singing and clapping the rhythms.
C. The choristers sing and arrange mixed-up rhythm cards of a known song or phrase in the correct order and then clap and sing the entire rhythm.
D. The singers write down simple rhythmic dictations after you:
    1. Count or speak rhythm names from patterns you have written on the board for the singers to copy.
    2. Count or speak rhythm names while clapping.
    3. Only clap.
    4. Play patterns on the piano or another instrument.
E. Ask your singers to analyze and find known patterns in a composition from the ensemble's repertoire.
F. Add known melodies to known rhythms and read from the board and choral score with both counting/rhythm names and solfa and/or letter names.
G. Create strategies where singers sight-read known rhythms in the ensemble's current repertoire.
H. Ask singers to improvise four- or eight-beat rhythms using the counting or syllables they know.

FURTHER PRACTICE OF MELODY, RHYTHM, AND PIANO

If your singers have ample passing time between classes or hang out in the choral room early in the morning or well after class is over, then you have probably heard more versions of "Heart and Soul" and "Lean on Me" than you ever cared

159

to. You can encourage your singers to practice what they are learning in their rehearsals during this downtime by placing sheets of music and instructions on the piano rack that direct the singers' enjoyment of the piano. Depending on the technology available, you can also provide the information on a computer screen or an overhead projector.

For example:

    A. Find F on the piano. Play it and sing as d.

    B. Sing this song with:

        1. Solfa.

        2. Letter names.

        3. Counting.

    C. Play this song on the piano.

    D. Can you find other places on the piano to play this song?

SCORES QUOTED

MELODY

Do-Re-Mi

"May Song"
Franz Schubert
Edited by Doreen Rao
Two-part treble
Boosey & Hawkes
OCTB6578

"Beside Thy Cradle Here I Stand"
Johann Sebastian Bach
Novello and Company

"Celtic Cradle Song"
Traditional Irish song
Arranged by Robert I. Hugh
Unison treble (with a second voice part added at end) and piano
Hal Leonard Corporation
08744430

"Three French Folk Songs"
Arranged by Geoffrey Edwards
Two equal voices and piano
Heritage Music Press
15/1008

Sol

"Circle 'round the Moon," from *Reflections of Youth*
Mark Hierholzer
Two-part treble voices with piano accompaniment
Colla Voce Music
21-20537

"Sleep My Baby" ("Suo-Gan")
Welsh
Arranged by Alec Rowley
Unison
Boosey & Hawkes
OCTB5449

"Kyrie"
Based on the Largo of Symphony no. 9, op. 95
Antonín Dvořák
Arranged by Ruth Elaine Schram
For two-part or two soprano and alto voices, accompanied, with optional C instrument
Alfred Publishing Co.
17979

Fa

"Coffee Grows on White Oak Trees"
Arranged by Vernon Sanders
Two-part
Thomas House Publications
1C148405

"Dormi, Dormi"
Arranged by Mary Goetze
For unison treble voices and piano or harp
Boosey & Hawkes
OCT6128

Fa-Sol

"The Piglets' Christmas"
Arranged by Mary Goetz
Unison
Boosey & Hawkes
OCTB6402

"Over the Sea to Skye"
Arranged by Joyce Eilers
Two-part treble
Jenson Publications
402-15012

"Glory to God"
Giovanni Pergolesi
Arranged by Michael Burkhardt
Two-part voices, two C instruments (optional) and keyboard
Morningstar Music Publishers
50-1450

La

"Things I Learned from a Cow"
Valerie Showers Crescenz
Two-part with piano
Alliance Music Publications
AMP 0688

"American Folk Rhapsody"
Arranged by Linda Steen Spevacek
Two-part chorus and piano
Heritage Music Press
15/1213H

"Songs of a Summer Afternoon"
Traditional game song
Arranged by Emily Crocker
For three-part treble and piano
Hal Leonard Corporation
08753050

High Do

"The Sally Gardens"
Arranged by Benjamin Britten
Unison
Boosey & Hawkes
OCTB5448

163

"Sail Away"
Arranged by Susan Brumfield
For two soprano and two alto voices, a cappella
Colla Voce Music, Inc.
24-96370

Low La

"Things I Learned from a Cow"
Valerie Showers Crescenz
Two-part with piano
Alliance Music Publications
AMP 0688

"Born, Born in Bethlehem"
American spiritual
Arranged with additional music by Donald P. Moore (ASCAP)
Unison, optional two-part, accompanied
BriLee Music Publishing
BL365

Low Sol

"American Folk Rhapsody"
Arranged by Linda Steen Spevacek
Two-part chorus and piano
Heritage Music Press
15/1213H

"I Bought Me a Cat"
Traditional
Arranged by Linda Steen Spevacek
Two-part treble
Hal Leonard Corporation
0872815

"Chatter with the Angels"
Spiritual
Arranged by Charles Collins
Two-part treble voices and piano
Boosey & Hawkes
OCTB6795

Ti

"Friendship Song"
Czech canon
Edited and arranged by Doreen Rao
Four-part treble
Boosey & Hawkes
OCTB6616

"Kyrie Eleison"
Ron Kean
Two-part voices and piano
Pavane Publishing
08300224

"Ich Jauchze, ich Lache mit Schall" ("Laughing and Shouting for Joy")
Two-part treble
Johann Sebastian Bach
Edited by Doreeen Rao
Boosey & Hawkes
48004227

"Sound the Trumpet"
Henry Purcell
Two-part treble
Choral Public Domain Library (www.cpdl.org)

"An Invitation," from *Three Children's Songs*
Ralph Vaughn Williams
Oxford University Press
55.017

Natural Minor

"The Little Birch Tree"
Arranged by Mary Goetze
Unison voices with piano and optional recorder or flute
Boosey & Hawkes
48003970

"Old Abram Brown," from *Friday Afternoons*
Benjamin Britten
Unison voices and piano
Boosey & Hawkes
48011758

"A Daffodil, Too"
B. Wayne Bisbee
Unison voices and piano
Santa Barbara Music Publishing
SBMP 370

RHYTHM

"Mrs. Jenny Wren"
Arthur Baynon
Unison
Boosey & Hawkes
OCUB6117

"Beside Thy Cradle Here I Stand"
Johann Sebastian Bach
Novello and Company

"Deux Poules Françaises" ("Hopi, Hop")
French children's song
Arranged by Sheila Donahue
Two-part children's choir with piano
Alliance Music Publications
AMP 0310

"Fum, Fum, Fum"
Spanish dance carol
Arranged by Judy Herrington and Sara Glick
Two-part with piano and percussion
Pavane Publishing
P1170

"A New Year Carol," from *Friday Afternoons*
Music by Benjamin Britten
Unison voices and piano
Boosey & Hawkes
48011758

"Kokoleoko"
Liberian folk song
Additional words and music by Mary Donnelly (ASCAP)
Arranged by George L. O. Strid (ASCAP)
Two-part, accompanied
Warner Bros. Publications U.S.
SVM02049

"Velvet Shoes"
Randall Thompson
Unison voices and piano
Schirmer Music Co.
2526

"Al Shlosha D'varim"
Allan E. Kaplan
Two-part treble with piano
Boosey & Hawkes
48004534

"S'vivon"
Traditional Hebrew song
Arranged by Betty Bertaux
Two soprano and two alto voices, a cappella
Boosey & Hawkes
OCTB6840

"Aussie Animals"
Original words and music and arrangement by David Lawrence
Unison or two-part with piano
Warner Bros. Publications

"Old Joe Clark"
Vocal arrangement by Judy Herrington
Accompaniment by Sara Glick
Two-part treble with piano
Pavane Publishing
P1017

"Gloria"
Franz Joseph Haydn, arranged by Patrick M. Liebergen
Three-part treble with piano
Alfred Publishing Co.
17800

"Ezekiel and David"
Traditional spirituals
Arranged by Sally K. Albrecht
Alfred Publishing Co.
31011

"Sandmännchen"
Johannes Brahms
Public Domain Choral Library (www.cpdl.org)

"Spring" from *Three Children's Songs*
R. Vaughan Williams
Unison voices and piano
Oxford University Press
55.015

168

"Old Joe Clark"
Vocal arrangement by Judy Herrington
Accompaniment by Sara Glick
Two-part treble
Pavane Publishing
P1017

"Goin' to Boston"
American folk song
Arranged by Shirley W. McRae
Two-part treble voices with flute and keyboard accompaniment
Colla Voce Music
21-20546

CREDITS

LESSON 1

"Celtic Cradle Song"
Traditional Irish song, arranged by Robert Hugh
Copyright © 2006 by Hal Leonard Corporation
International copyright secured
All rights reserved

"Three French Folk Songs"
Arranged by Geoffrey Edwards
© MCMXCIII Heritage Music Press
All rights reserved
Used by permission

LESSON 2

"May Song"
By Franz Schubert, edited by Doreen Rao
© Copyright by Boosey & Hawkes, Inc.
Reprinted by permission

LESSON 3A

"Mrs. Jenny Wren"
By Arthur Baynon; Text by Rodney Bennett
© Copyright 1953 by Boosey & Co. Ltd.
Reprinted by permission

"Deux Poule Francaises" ("Hopi, Hop")
French children's song, arranged by Sheila Donahue
Copyright © 1998 Alliance Music Publications, Inc.
Used by permission

LESSON 3B

"Fum, Fum, Fum"
Arranged by Judith Herrington and Sara Glick
© Copyright 2000 Pavane Publishing
Used by permission
All rights reserved

LESSON 5A

"Sleep My Baby" ("Suo-Gan")
By Alec Rowley
© Copyright 1954 by Boosey & Co. Ltd.
Reprinted by permission

"Circle 'round the Moon" (21-20537)
Music by Mark Hierholzer
Copyright © 1997 Plymouth Music Co., Inc.
Copyright © 2000 Transferred Colla Voce Music, Inc.
www.collavoce.com

"Kyrie"
By Antonín Dvořák
Arranged by Ruth Elaine Schram
© 1998 by Alfred Music Publishing Co., Inc.
All rights reserved

LESSON 5B

"The Piglets' Christmas"
By Mary Goetze
© Copyright Boosey & Hawkes, Inc.
Reprinted by permission

"Over the Sea to Skye"
Words by Robert Louis Stevenson
Music by Annie McLeod
Copyright © 1980 by Jenson Publications
International copyright secured
All rights reserved

"Glory to God"
By Giovanni Pergolesi, arranged by Michael Burkhardt
Copyright © 1990 by Birnamwood Publications (ASCAP)
A division of MorningStar Music Publishers, Inc., St. Louis, MO
Used by permission

LESSON 6

"A New Year Carol"
By Benjamin Britten
© Copyright 1936 by Boosey & Co Ltd.
Reprinted by Permission

"Kokoleoko"
Additional words and music by Mary Donnelly
Arranged by George L. O. Strid
© 2002 STUDIO 224
All rights assigned to and controlled by Alfred Music Publishing Co., Inc.
All rights reserved

LESSON 7

"Velvet Shoes"
By Randall Thompson
© 1960 by E. C. Schirmer Music Co., a division of ECS Publishing
www.ecspub.com
Used by permission

"Al Shlosha D'varim"
By Allan E. Kaplan
© Copyright by Boosey & Hawkes, Inc.
Reprinted by permission

LESSON 8

"Things I Learned from a Cow"
By Valerie Showers Crescenz
Copyright © 2007 Alliance Music Publications, Inc.
Used by permission

"Songs of a Summer Afternoon"
Traditional, arranged by Emily Crocker
Copyright © 2011 by Hal Leonard Corporation
International copyright secured
All rights reserved

LESSON 9

"Dormi, Dormi"
By Mary Goetze
© Copyright 1984 by Boosey & Hawkes, Inc.
Reprinted by permission

171

LESSON 10

"Aussie Animals"
Words and music by David Lawrence
© 2003 STUDIO 224
All rights assigned to and controlled by Alfred Music Publishing Co., Inc.

LESSON 11

"The Sally Gardens"
By Benjamin Britten; Text by William Yeats
© Copyright 1943 by Boosey & Co. Ltd.
Reprinted by permission

"Sail Away" (24-96370)
Arranged by Susan Brumfield
Copyright © 2011 Colla Voce Music, Inc.
www.collavoce.com

LESSON 12

"Old Joe Clark"
Arranged by Judy Herrington and Sara Glick
© Copyright 1991 Pavane Publishing
Used by permission

"Gloria"
Music by Franz Joseph Haydn
Arranged by Patrick M. Liebgergen
© 1994 Bel Win-Mills Publishing Corp.
A Division of Alfred Music Publishing Co., Inc.

"Ezekiel and David"
Arranged by Sally K. Albrecht
© 2008 by Alfred Music Publishing Co., Inc.

LESSON 13

"Things I Learned from a Cow"
By Valerie Showers Crescenz
Copyright © 2007 Alliance Music Publications, Inc.
Used by permission

LESSON 14

"Friendship Song"
By Doreen Rao
© Copyright by Boosey & Hawkes, Inc.
Reprinted by permission

"Kyrie for Communion" (from *Kyrie Eleison, Let Us Break Bread Together*)
Music by Ron Kean
© Copyright 1999, 2005 Pavane Publishing
Used by permission
All rights reserved

"Duet from Cantata no. 15"
By Johann Sebastian Bach; Edited by Doreen Rao
© Copyright by Boosey & Hawkes, Inc.
Reprinted by permission

"An Invitation" (no. 3 of *Three Children's Songs*)
Music by Ralph Vaughn Williams
© Oxford University Press 1930
Extract reproduced by permission
All rights reserved

LESSON 15

"Spring" (no. 3 of *Three Children's Songs*)
Music by Ralph Vaughn Williams
© Oxford University Press 1930
Extract reproduced by permission
All rights reserved

LESSON 16

"Old Joe Clark"
Arranged by Judy Herrington and Sara Glick
© Copyright 1991 Pavane Publishing
Used by permission
All rights reserved

"Goin' to Boston" (21-20546)
Arranged by Shirley W. McRae
Copyright © 1999 Plymouth Music Co., Inc.
Copyright © 2000 transferred Colla Voce Music, Inc.
www.collavoce.com

LESSON 17

"American Folk Rhapsody"
Arranged by Linda Steen Spevacek
© MCMXCV Heritage Music Press

"I Bought Me a Cat"
Traditional American folk song, arranged by Linda Steen Spevacek
Copyright © 1989 by Hal Leonard Corporation

"Chatter with the Angels"
By Charles Collins
© Copyright by Boosey & Hawkes, Inc.

LESSON 18

"The Little Birch Tree"
By Mary Goetze
© Copyright 1984 by Boosey & Hawkes, Inc.

"Old Abram Brown"
By Benjamin Britten
© Copyright 1936 by Boosey & Co Ltd.

"A Daffodil, Too"
By B. Wayne Bisbee
© Copyright 2000 by Santa Barbara Music Publishing

ABOUT THE AUTHOR

David J. Xiques is professor of music in the School of Music and Dance at San Francisco State University, where he teaches ear training and musicianship classes and directs the University Chorus and Chamber Singers. His teaching experience includes fifteen years in K–12 choral, junior and high school band, and general music classes. A Kodály specialist, he teaches at the Kodály Summer Certification Program at New York University. In addition, he is a professional singer, tenor, with the San Francisco Symphony Chorus, where he serves as assistant chorus director. He is a frequent choral clinician and presenter at professional music conferences.

As assistant chorus director of the San Francisco Symphony Chorus, he prepared the Grammy Award–winning ensemble for performances of Mozart's *Mass in C Minor* for Ingo Metzmacher, conductor. He also prepared the Chorus for the North American premier of John Adams's *Flowering Tree* for Maestro Adams, who conducted the performances.

His work as a chorus director can be heard in a recording of *Printemps* on the CD *Debussy Rediscovered, Premier Orchestral Recordings*, released in 2000 under the Arabesque label. He worked closely with the conductor Emil de Cou, music director of the San Francisco Ballet Orchestra, in recreating Debussy's original version of *Printemps* by restoring Debussy's wordless chorus to the orchestration. Before this time *Printemps* had been heard only in an orchestral version.

Xiques earned his M.M. in Music Education with Kodály Emphasis degree from Holy Names University in Oakland, California, where he was a member of the faculty, and B.S. in Music Education from Millersville University in Millersville, Pennsylvania. He studied ear training and musicianship extensively with Erzsébet Hegyi of the Liszt Academy in Budapest, and conducting with Vance George of the San Francisco Symphony Chorus, as well as members of the 1995 Chorus America faculty at Saranac Lake, New York.

Printed in Great Britain
by Amazon

16337408R00109